Additional praise for *The OKRs Field Book*

"Ben's first book, *Objectives & Key Results: Driving Focus, Alignment, and Engagement with OKRs*, was well received by my teams and got us started using OKRs over two years ago. I am now ready to take OKRs to the division level, and Ben's *OKRs Field Book* gives me a solid path forward to implement goal-setting based on outcomes, not just output. This book is going to be what I read each time I feel that I have lost my way in implementing OKRs. The 'coach takeaways' and 'chapter exercises' alone are worth the price of the book."

—Phil Clark, PhD, Technical Director, 3M

"*The OKRs Field Book* has made an immediate and positive impact on how we deliver OKRs coaching across the firm. The combination of a proven methodology and Ben's deep understanding of what it takes to be a great coach make this book an invaluable resource for both internal and external OKR coaches."

—Peter Kerr, Managing Director and Cofounder of Auxin OKR Ltd, United Kingdom

"This field book made our OKRs journey richer. It enables our coaches to implement OKRs with their clients. Ben's work quite literally directly benefits all our clients, making them more focused and ultimately more successful. You won't find a better practical guide to OKRs coaching anywhere."

—James Hughes, Growth Coach, GROW Business Coaching, South Africa

"Ben Lamorte is THE most deeply experienced external OKR coach in the business, having been at it since 2010. *The OKRs Field Book* is an up-to-date compendium of where the OKRs field is in 2022, and it is the first OKRs book written especially for OKRs coaches. This book belongs on any OKRs practitioner's bookshelf—you'll learn a lot!"

—Daniel J. Montgomery, Managing Director, Agile Strategies

The OKRs Field Book

The OKRs Field Book

A Step-by-Step Guide for Objectives and Key Results Coaches

BEN LAMORTE

WILEY

Published by John Wiley & Sons, Inc., Hoboken, New Jersey.
Published simultaneously in Canada.

For general information on our other products and services or for technical support, please contact our Customer Care Department within the United States at (800) 762-2974, outside the United States at (317) 572-3993 or fax (317) 572-4002.

Wiley also publishes its books in a variety of electronic formats. Some content that appears in print may not be available in electronic formats. For more information about Wiley products, visit our website at www.wiley.com.

Library of Congress Cataloging-in-Publication Data:

Names: Lamorte, Ben, author.
Title: The OKRs field book : a step-by-step guide for objectives and key
   results coaches / Ben Lamorte.
Description: Hoboken, NJ : Wiley, [2022] | Includes index.
Identifiers: LCCN 2021046899 (print) | LCCN 2021046900 (ebook) | ISBN
   9781119816423 (paperback) | ISBN 9781119816447 (adobe pdf) | ISBN
   9781119816430 (epub)
Subjects: LCSH: Executive coaching. | Teams in the workplace.
Classification: LCC HD30.4 .L34 2022 (print) | LCC HD30.4 (ebook) | DDC
   658.4/07124—dc23/eng/20211109
LC record available at https://lccn.loc.gov/2021046899
LC ebook record available at https://lccn.loc.gov/2021046900

Cover Design: Wiley
Cover Image: Courtesy of Ben Lamorte

SKY10033109_020722

To my father, Mario,
for being the constant force that
guided me to find my path
during our time together.

Contents

Preface

N 2015, I WAS lucky enough to meet Paul Niven, a leading author on strategy and performance management. We wrote *Objectives and Key Results: Driving Focus, Alignment, and Engagement with OKRs* in 2016. That book was based on my early success as an OKRs coach and featured interviews with several of my clients. In 2016, I was still a student discovering how best to deploy OKRs. In this book, I am the teacher. I teach you to master the art of OKRs coaching based on my experience coaching 200 organizations and mentoring dozens of coaches. Here is the story of how I ended up writing this book.

In late 2018, shortly after *Measure What Matters* hit the market, coaches from around the world started reaching out to me for guidance. These coaches were new to using objectives and key results, but they did not ask me about the basics of OKRs. That information was already covered in the existing literature. They wanted to know how to be an effective OKRs coach – everything from how best to design an OKRs coaching engagement to how to facilitate coaching sessions at each step of the OKRs cycle.

In 2019, I got consistent feedback from other coaches that my guidance was working. With countless organizations launching OKRs coach certificate programs, I was compelled to develop a certificate program of my own. However, I quickly realized that the foundation for an OKRs coach certificate program was not in place. There was no definitive book written for coaches by OKRs coaches. As my colleagues kept claiming that "Ben Lamorte has more OKRs coaching experience than anyone on the planet," I decided to take on the challenge.

In 2020, I allocated most of my time to writing this book. My confidence in this project skyrocketed when 20 people attended an OKRs Coach Network webinar series previewing each chapter. These coaches provided feedback that validated the book's content, including the first definition of "OKRs coaching."

In early 2021, I self-published a draft of this book. I was delighted when Wiley offered to publish this definitive first edition. I believe that this first edition of *The OKRs Field Book* marks the birth of OKRs coaching as a formal discipline. I hope that it will be used as part of OKRs coaching certification programs and that future editions will feature contributions from you, the next generation of OKRs coaches.

—Ben Lamorte, OKRs Coach
San Anselmo, California

Acknowledgments

THIS BOOK IS WRITTEN for OKRs coaches. While many coaches contributed, this book would not be possible without Jeff Walker and Christina Wodkte. Jeff leveraged the OKRs framework at Oracle in the 1980s as EVP, founder, and general manager, Applications Division and as the CFO. He introduced me to OKRs and in 2010 became my first professional mentor. Jeff challenged me to get out of my comfort zone and inspired me to follow my passion as an OKRs coach.

While this is the first book dedicated to OKRs coaching, Christina Wodtke's *Radical Focus* was the first book dedicated to OKRs in general. My collaborations with Christina, along with countless meetings comparing coaching trends and best practices greatly inform this field book. Thanks also to John Doerr, Rick Klau, Kuang Yang, Paul Niven, Dan Montgomery, and Felipe Castro for helping shape the burgeoning OKRs coaching field.

I am indebted to my editors, Dean Burrell and Sheck Cho, for helping structure and refine this book. I thank my designer, Chris Vacano, for the Friday afternoon working sessions that translated my ideas about OKRs coaching into effective visuals.

Thanks to Kathryn Britton, Bess Keller, and Brian Branagan for facilitating a series of writers' workshops. Your support kept this book project moving forward and introduced me to a network of authors. Authors providing especially valuable feedback and support include Jane Egerton-Idehen, Jane Anderson, Jen Grace Baron, and Senia Maymin. Thanks for making me a better writer!

Thanks to the OKRs.com team for supporting me throughout the writing process. Mandy Hill and Carter Coleman helped collect feedback. Dikran Yapoujian, the first coach to join the OKRs.com team, helped validate the three phases of an OKRs coaching engagement introduced in this book. Dikran's success as an OKRs coach provided me with the confidence – and audacity – that I needed to write this book. Thanks also to Sid Ghatak, Karen Schroeder, Catherine Chen, Gerri Vereen, Jean-Luc Koning, Ana Venosa, Nash Billimoria, Omid Akhavan, Sundara Nagarajan, and Carol Mase.

Thanks to the OKRs Coach Network founding members for providing feedback in our book preview webinar series. In addition to USA-based coaches, founding members of the network include coaches based in Bangladesh, Brazil, Chile, China, France, Germany, Greece, Hungary, India, Indonesia, Iran, Malaysia, Netherlands, Poland, South Africa, Spain, Switzerland, Thailand, and the United Kingdom.

Finally, I'd like to thank my parents, Suellen and Mario (posthumously), my wife, Ariana, and my two children, Toby and Lizzie, for their love and support.

Introduction

THIS IS THE FIRST book dedicated to *OKRs coaching*. This is not an introduction to OKRs. I wrote this book for external and internal coaches looking to take their OKRs coaching skills to the next level.

If you provide OKRs coaching services to your clients, you are an external OKRs coach. This book speaks directly to you. It enables you to better support your clients as they launch OKRs or improve their existing OKRs program.

If you work at an organization that is using (or about to use) OKRs and are tasked with helping your organization deploy OKRs effectively, you are an internal OKRs coach. Although this book addresses external coaches, internal coaches can also benefit.

To get the most from this book, you should be familiar with books such as *Radical Focus*, by Christina Wodtke; *Objectives and Key Results*, a book I co-authored with Paul Niven; and *Measure What Matters*, by John Doerr. These three books provide an excellent introduction to OKRs. They cover the first layer of information, such as the history and benefits of implementing OKRs, success stories, and the distinction between an objective and a key result. However, OKRs coaches want to go deeper. My colleagues and clients are asking for the answers to these deeper questions. Here are 10 examples (answers to these questions are included in the appendix):

1. How can we scale OKRs across a large organization with hundreds of departments?
2. How can we set team-level OKRs to ensure cross-functional alignment rather than simply using the org chart to define the teams that will set OKRs?
3. How can infrastructure teams such as legal, human resources, and finance benefit from OKRs?

4. How do we integrate OKRs into our performance management system?
5. How do OKRs compare with KPIs?
6. When do OKRs *not* add value?
7. How do we ensure that OKRs reflect team thinking rather than orders from the boss?
8. How do we avoid OKRs that look like a "to-do list"?
9. What if some employees do not see how they contribute to company-level OKRs?
10. How do I facilitate an executive workshop to draft top-level OKRs?

Although there are no magic answers to these questions that work for every organization, this book gives you the tools to answer these and other questions in the context of your client's situation. It's called a *field book* because it focuses on nitty-gritty advice, tips, and tools to help you apply OKRs in the field with confidence. For example, this book includes a sample handout that you can use to draft OKRs, sample worksheets that organizations use to track their OKRs, and sample agendas with tips for facilitating OKRs workshops.

HOW THIS BOOK IS ORGANIZED AND HOW TO BEST USE IT

The five chapters in this book provide a step-by-step guide to support your client's OKRs program. Though this book may be read from cover to cover, it is best used as a reference guide that you can come back to as you master each step of an OKRs coaching engagement. Each chapter begins with the skills it teaches and ends with an exercise to transfer content from theory into practice. Exercises are your opportunity to critically reflect on your OKRs coaching approach. They also help you internalize the concepts in this book so you can bring OKRs coaching to your clients in your own way. If you're an active OKRs coach, consider completing the reflection exercise at the end of this introduction right now.

Chapter 1 is the foundation for the entire book. It offers an analysis of why OKRs coaching is vital right now and features the first collective definition of OKRs coaching.

Chapter 2 summarizes the nine roles, three phases, and recommended duration of an OKRs coaching engagement. Roles include (1) external OKRs coach, (2) executive sponsor, (3) OKRs project lead, (4) OKRs coordinator, (5) human resources lead, (6) team lead, (7) team member, (8) key result champion, and (9) internal OKRs coach. Phases include

(1) deployment coaching, (2) training, and (3) cycle coaching. This book gives coaches a detailed guide for each phase.

Chapter 3 is the playbook for Phase 1, deployment coaching, in which you help your client define their deployment parameters. As an OKRs coach, it is imperative that you absorb and master this content. Think of these parameters as answers to the questions you need to have in place before rolling out OKRs. There are 10 universal parameters to confirm with every client:

1. At what level will we set OKRs – company, team, individual?
2. How many OKRs will we set? How will we balance internal and external objectives?
3. How will we score OKRs? How will we update progress?
4. How long is an OKRs cycle?
5. What are the three types of key results? Are milestones appropriate?
6. Where will we draft, publish, and track OKRs?
7. How will OKRs relate to performance reviews?
8. How are OKRs different from KPIs?
9. How will we ensure that OKRs are aligned?
10. How will we ensure most OKRs originate "bottom-up"?

With these parameters in place, you can design and deliver training.

Chapter 4 is the playbook for Phase 2, training. You'll find the three types of training workshops proven to be most effective along with actual agendas from the field. Workshops create enthusiasm and often yield a solid set of draft OKRs. However, to be an effective OKRs coach, you must stick around to coach your client through at least one OKRs cycle.

Chapter 5 is the playbook for coaching your client through the three steps in an OKRs cycle:

Step 1: Set and align OKRs.
Step 2: Check in and monitor progress.
Step 3: Reflect and reset.

In addition to an analysis of each step and questions to ask along the way, this chapter includes excerpts from actual coaching sessions and a case study that follows an OKR through each step of the cycle.

The epilogue previews content available exclusively to members of the OKRs Coach Network.[1] This content includes: (1) the questions OKRs coaches ask, (2) a sample drafting handout you can use with clients right away, and (3) sample ineffective and effective key results. We end the book with two stories that reflect lessons learned with vital implications for OKRs coaches. With this overview out of the way, let's get to know each other.

OKRs ORIGIN STORIES

When I met Christina Wodtke, author of *Radical Focus*, she asked me to describe how and why I got into OKRs. I found the conversation immensely valuable. It was the first time I reflected on why I became an OKRs coach. Christina suggested that sharing OKRs origin stories is a great place to start when meeting other OKRs coaches. So, whenever I meet an OKRs coach colleague, I begin with origin stories. I will share mine now and hope you will share yours.[2]

My OKRs origin story goes back to graduate school. As a twenty-something working on my doctoral degree in management science and engineering at Stanford University in the late 1990s, I completed my coursework and was about to start research for my dissertation. Faced with several more years of living on a teaching assistant's income and the rising cost of housing around the Stanford campus, I decided to drop out of graduate school and get a job. I took a position with a leading management consulting firm. But I was desperate for approval from Michael Fehling, my academic advisor. I asked Michael, "Is it OK for me to take this job? Do you approve?" to which Michael replied,

"As long as you have time for critical reflection, you'll do great."

Michael was so right. In the first year, the consulting firm had me working 80 hours per week – I did not have time to reflect. I spent countless hours editing PowerPoint slides, linking tables in databases, and building macros in spreadsheets. I just kept doing whatever I was asked to do. I developed practical skills, but I had no time for critical reflection. So, I left and joined a well-funded dot-com startup.

After a decade of working, first as a management consultant and later for dot-com startups, Jeffrey L. Walker introduced me to OKRs in 2010. Jeff was the founder of Oracle Applications and later served as CFO during Oracle's rapid growth in the late 1980s. Jeff used OKRs at Oracle. Importantly, he taught me how to communicate more effectively by emphasizing the desired result rather than listing out all the projects and tasks that are on my to-do list. With Jeff's guidance, I began working with the OKRs model in 2011.

My first paid OKRs engagement began with a request to "support the creation of metrics and performance dashboards for dozens of departments across several business units." My client sent me a 20-page strategy document packed with metrics, strategic pillars, and priorities. After reading the document, I felt lost. So, I reread the document several times and translated it into the OKRs framework. When I presented the strategy as a set of four OKRs on a single page to the CEO and CFO, they asked me to create the exact same OKRs document for each business unit and department.

The critical thinking that occurred during my first wave of OKRs coaching sessions with this client marked a turning point in my career. For the first time, I was engaged in a work activity that could change the game. Nearly all 40 managers in my first round of paid OKRs coaching gave me feedback that was 10 times more positive than any feedback I had ever received. I was onto something big. Rather than the old model of asking questions in order to get data to populate a financial model for their boss, I introduced a different set of questions – questions such managers need to be asking themselves. Here are some examples:

- Why does our team exist?
- What is the most important objective for our team to focus on this quarter?
- How will we know we've achieved the objective?

These questions are the very same questions Jeff Walker asked back when he introduced me to OKRs. They shook my world.[3] They forced the critical reflection that Professor Fehling advocated. I realized that great mentors and coaches tend to emphasize asking questions over giving advice.

As there were no job openings for "OKRs Coach," I settled for the next best thing – I joined Betterworks, an OKRs software company. I felt that joining the five-person team at Betterworks, which was in the prefunded startup phase, was the big break I was looking for. Just a few months after I accepted the job offer, the legendary Silicon Valley investor and OKRs evangelist, John Doerr, agreed to invest $12 million in our young company – his largest A-Round since Google!

I provided training to Betterworks customers to help them define and load OKRs into an early version of our software. I took roughly two days with one client to train several teams. While the feedback from this client was quite positive, the Betterworks CEO was not happy. Software companies get big valuations by delivering scalable technologies, not time-consuming services. Betterworks expected me to train all teams in several hours, not to train some of the teams in several days!

So, I left Betterworks in 2014, started OKRs.com, and decided to focus on OKRs coaching. While I felt as if I was heading in a good direction, I faced three challenges: (1) I lacked a steady source of income, (2) it was not easy to find clients looking for OKRs coaching, and (3) I had no marketing budget. At that time, almost no one had even heard of OKRs, so I decided to postpone my dreams and take on consulting work unrelated to OKRs. Something didn't feel right, so I turned back to Jeff Walker.

Jeff:	What is the one thing that you do best that also has significant business value?
Me:	OKRs coaching
Jeff:	How many hours per week are you doing this OKRs coaching on average?
Me:	Three or four
Jeff:	Why not make that 30 to 40?
Me:	But there's no way to do that. My consulting clients are paying me to build financial models.
Jeff:	Stop doing that other stuff and start focusing on OKRs coaching. If you can't get paid to do it, just do it for free. Make it your goal to do as many sessions, free or paid, as possible. If you are adding business value, people will start paying for it. And, if you can deliver significant value, you'll find out just how big the market really is.

After this brief interaction, I embraced Jeff's challenge. I started offering free OKRs coaching to anyone who would give me an hour of their time. I recorded dozens of these free coaching sessions. I reviewed each recording and transcribed certain sections. I analyzed where we got stuck or made breakthroughs using the Left-Hand Column (LHC) reflection exercise that Professor Fehling introduced to me at Stanford.[4] It took me a while, but I ultimately confirmed the value of OKRs coaching.

By mid-2014, I was 100% focused on OKRs coaching. I managed to have a slight profit in 2015, and 2016 was my first truly profitable year as well as the year I coauthored a book on OKRs. By 2018, I could barely meet the demand for coaching services. So, I expanded my team to include Dikran Yapoujian.[5] Building off the success with Dikran, I started mentoring other OKRs coaches. By 2019, OKRs coaches from around the world were approaching me for advice on how to provide OKRs coaching to their clients.

This book contains the foundational content you need to be an effective OKRs coach. It is based on OKRs coaching projects with hundreds of organizations over the past decade, as well as input from the OKRs coach community. The use of "I" refers to me, Ben Lamorte. The use of "we" refers to the entire OKRs.com coaching team.

 ## TRENDS OKRs COACHES SHOULD KNOW

While the 2016 book, *Objectives and Key Results*, is still relevant today, we've since learned a lot and seen some big changes. Here are six developing trends that we believe you should know before we get into the nuts and bolts of OKRs coaching:

1. ***Organizations are postponing discussions of setting OKRs at the individual-person level.*** Back in 2016, nearly half of our clients wanted to get going with company-level, team-level, and individual-level OKRs right from the start.[6] Now, most organizations are embracing the notion that we should begin by defining OKRs at the highest possible level and pilot OKRs with several teams prior to even considering setting OKRs at the individual-person level. Nearly all of our clients agree that we should never require all individuals to define OKRs. This is a great development from our perspective. Chapter 3 analyzes the level at which to set OKRs in an organization.

2. ***Organizations are allowing more time to deploy OKRs and embracing a* crawl-walk-run *approach.*** In 2016, quite a few organizations asked for a brief OKRs project that might include a call or two along with an onsite training workshop without ongoing OKRs coaching. Now, nearly everyone looking for help with OKRs is demanding an

ongoing support program to ensure that their organization succeeds with OKRs over the course of at least one complete cycle. Chapter 2 explains how we arrived at 8 to 12 months as the ideal duration for an OKRs coaching engagement.

3. ***The definition of OKRs as a "critical thinking framework" is resonating even with organizations that do not formally adopt OKRs as their goal-setting model.***[7] Some of our clients are bringing the discipline of OKRs coaching to improve their existing, non-OKRs goal-setting systems. In fact, several of our more established clients have goal-setting systems such as KPIs, MBOs, and/or balanced scorecards in place already, but they feel something is missing. They want to introduce OKRs, but they feel introducing another system could be a step backward, based on a legitimate concern that adding more acronyms and jargon to their existing goal-setting system could increase overhead. Nonetheless, these organizations are asking us to train their staff to focus more on outcomes, connect their work to strategy, or even to just get better at writing goals in general.

   In these cases, we bring OKRs coaching into organizations that choose not to formally deploy OKRs. We explain to the staff that as OKRs coaches, we ask structured questions designed to improve their existing goal-setting process. We ask fundamental OKRs questions such as:
   - Why is this objective so important now?
   - How will you know you've achieved the objective by the end of the quarter?
   - What is the intended outcome of the task?

   These questions force their staff to engage in critical reflection and inevitably help optimize their existing goal-setting system, even though we may not be naming it *OKRs*. When working with such clients, we provide ad-hoc coaching rather than taking the phased approach outlined in Chapters 3, 4, and 5.

4. ***The number of OKRs that an organization defines is trending down.*** Back in 2011, we often heard "5 +/− 2" as the guidance for the optimal number of objectives an organization should set. This translates to three as the minimum, five as typical, and seven as the recommended maximum. By 2016, most of our clients targeted three to five objectives, each with three to five key results. As of 2020, nearly all of our clients defined at most three objectives, each with just two to four key results. We consider this a good development, as OKRs are often intended to drive focus.

5. ***"Objective descriptions" are replaced with "Why now?"*** Back in 2016, we recommended including an "objective description" after each objective.[8] This confused our clients, and not everyone adopted the recommendation. By mid-2018, all of our clients adopted "Why now?" in place of objective descriptions. They align on three to five sentences that explain why the objective is so important right now. The emphasis on "Why now?" tends to educate and motivate the workforce. This step ensures alignment on the essence of the objective before taking on the time-consuming process of drafting key results.

   Beginning with "Why now?" is an excellent opportunity to add value as a coach. Several of our clients report that getting clear about why each objective is so important right now is the biggest benefit of their OKRs program. Leaders often announce OKRs by presenting the objective and the analysis of "Why now?" on a full slide before presenting key results.

6. ***OKRs cycles are shifting to four months.*** The default OKRs cycle time is still a quarter. However, beginning in 2019, nearly half of our clients adopted four-month cycle times to avoid problems due to holidays and the quarterly crunch. Organizations on a quarterly cycle typically announce their Q1 OKRs in mid- or even late February. This gives them just a few weeks before it's time to draft Q2 OKRs. They often experience another delay in July due to summer vacations. In addition to holiday-related delays, they feel pressure from the quarterly crunch.

   The sales team is often focused on closing deals near the end of a quarter. Other teams such as finance may be swamped with closing the books as a quarter begins. Introducing another quarterly process with more work can be overwhelming, exacerbating the quarterly crunch. Teams making the move from a three-month to a four-month cycle report a preference for three OKRs cycles each year rather than four.

This book elaborates on these six trends and more. As noted earlier, each section concludes with an exercise. If you'd like to skip this exercise and read Chapter 1, that's fine. However, the exercise below comes first for a reason. This is your chance to share your origin story and what led you to pick up this book.

NOTES

1. To learn more about the network, see the URL: www.okrscoach.network.
2. For details on how to share your story, see the exercise at the end of this introduction.
3. Refer to "Questions OKRs Coaches Ask" in the epilogue for more OKRs questions.
4. For more on the Left-Hand Column exercise, see the end of Chapter 1.
5. For more on Dikran, see the Contributor Bios at the end of this book as well as his coaching tips in Chapter 5.
6. The motivation for starting OKRs at the company, team, and individual levels was inspired by the 2014 Google Ventures Workshop Recording in which Rick Klau explains that OKRs exist at three levels. Subsequently, in November 2017, Klau clarified via Twitter: "6/ Skip individual OKRs altogether. Especially for younger, smaller companies. They're redundant. Focus on company and team-level OKRs." So, it is no surprise that the message to delay or even "skip individual-level OKRs altogether" is now becoming the default approach.
7. This definition for OKRs is as follows: A critical thinking framework and ongoing discipline that seeks to ensure that employees work together, focusing effort to make measurable contributions.
8. Think of objective descriptions as "the rationale for being, like a note to the CEO justifying why this objective should exist." Source: Paul R. Niven and Ben Lamorte, *Objectives and Key Results: Driving Focus, Alignment, and Engagement with OKRs* (Hoboken, NJ: John Wiley & Sons, 2016), p. 68.

INTRODUCTION **EXERCISE**

What is your OKRs origin story?

Use the following prompts or simply write whatever comes to mind to reflect on your OKRs journey thus far.

Why do you want to be an OKRs coach?

How can you relate your experiences with coaches and/or mentors throughout your education and professional career with your OKRs coaching work?

Were you ever an OKRs coachee who received coaching from another OKRs coach?

What is the impact you want to make as an OKRs coach? How can we measure this impact?

Bonus: Send your OKRs story to Ben@OKRs.com, with "MY OKRS ORIGIN STORY" in the subject line. We can then begin a conversation and explore ways to collaborate.

1

What Is OKRs Coaching? Why Is It So Important Now?

By the end of this chapter, you will be able to . . .

- Describe why OKRs coaching demand is on the rise in the 2020s.
- Define *OKRs coaching*.
- Apply a reflection exercise to improve your OKRs coaching skills.

T HE MOST IMPORTANT THING I learned in graduate school was not part of the engineering curriculum. It was something I learned from Dennis Matthies, a lecturer in the 1990s at Stanford's Center for Teaching and Learning. As part of his Accelerated Learning course, Matthies explained that prior to embracing a new skill, you should reflect on why you've chosen to take on the challenge in the first place. He presented data and shared examples to back this up. It seems obvious to me now; learning is accelerated when we can clearly explain why we're putting in the time to develop new skills. So, building off Dennis's teachings, let's explore why now is the right time to develop OKRs coaching skills.

This chapter begins with a brief recap of the history of OKRs. It describes how OKRs coaching demand emerged in the 2010s and started growing exponentially in 2018 into a mainstream business practice across the globe. After presenting the definition of OKRs coaching, the chapter ends with excerpts from actual coaching sessions to make the definition more concrete. The goal of this first chapter is for you to clearly state why OKRs coaching is important right now and why you have chosen to develop your coaching skills.

CURRENT STATE OF OKRs AND WHY NOW IS THE TIME TO DEVELOP OKRs COACHING SKILLS

As context for the current state of OKRs, let's go back to where it all started. In the late 1970s, Andy Grove introduced OKRs as an evolution of Management by Objectives (MBOs). Grove was then the CEO of Intel. As key executives left the company, they spread the word on OKRs to emerging big players such as Oracle in the 1980s and Google in the 1990s. By 2010, dozens of tech companies in Silicon Valley were using OKRs as a system for defining and achieving their most important goals.[1] So, if OKRs had been around for nearly 50 years, why the sudden interest in OKRs in 2013? Short answer: Google.

In early 2013, Google Ventures partner Rick Klau shared a video on how Google was using OKRs.[2] The video was wildly popular. Its impact led to the first spike of interest in OKRs outside the Silicon Valley and, indeed, outside the tech world.

> @klau tweet: "My OKRs video just passed 150,000 views. That's about 149k more than I thought it'd get."

In 2014, when the CEO of Sears viewed Klau's video, he immediately rolled out OKRs across the entire organization. Sears Holding Company is not a tech company by anyone's definition. The introduction of OKRs at Sears exemplified its expanding popularity and is just one of many examples of the growth of OKRs across business sectors.

With the popularity of OKRs gaining traction, business leaders and management consultants from all over the world began approaching OKRs coaches for both coaching and support. In 2016, Christina Wodtke published *Radical Focus*, the first book dedicated to the topic of OKRs. Later, in 2016, the book *Objectives and Key Results*, by Niven and Lamorte, introduced the steps for deploying OKRs. This book offered case studies from organizations around the world, as the interest in OKRs was growing outside the United States. Both *Radical Focus* and *Objectives and Key Results* became essential reading for anyone interested in OKRs, and both were translated into several languages.

In 2017, I made multiple trips to China, where I partnered with Beisen, a leading HR software company based in Beijing. I delivered a series of OKRs training workshops in Beijing, Shanghai, and Shenzhen to certify 200 business leaders. During one of these trips to China, I was lucky enough to spend a couple days with executives at Huawei, one of China's leading technology companies. At Huawei, I met Kuang Yang, an OKRs expert who not only translated the OKRs book I coauthored, but also went on to write the first book dedicated to OKRs written in Chinese.[3] Kuang explained that the impact of Huawei's success with OKRs in China was comparable to the impact of Google's success with OKRs on tech companies in the United States.

By the end of 2017, OKRs were taking off across the globe. In addition to collaborating with organizations in China, I had clients based in Singapore, Australia, Poland, South Africa, France, Germany, Israel, India, Norway, the Netherlands, the United Kingdom, and Canada.

However, even in 2017 the demand for OKRs coaching was still nascent. In early 2018, I had roughly one call per week with a different company exploring OKRs. I continued to allocate a portion of my time to marketing efforts such as speaking on OKRs and posting content to The OKRs Blog on OKRs.com. But then 2018 happened.

The interest in OKRs started to grow exponentially after John Doerr's book on OKRs, *Measure What Matters*, hit the market in April of 2018. The stories in Doerr's book featured big names like Bono and Bill Gates. With a growing interest in OKRs came an increased demand for OKRs coaching. I shifted my focus exclusively to deliver OKRs coaching to my clients. I finally had the problem I always wanted: too many leads! We expect the global demand for OKRs coaching will continue to rise throughout the 2020s. Given that OKRs coaching is such a big deal, let's define it.

What Is OKRs Coaching?

To define what OKRs coaching is, let's begin by looking at what OKRs coaching is *not*. OKRs coaching is not consulting. Unlike consultants, who mostly advise their clients, coaches focus on inquiry.

The International Coaching Federation defines coaching as "partnering with clients in a thought-provoking and creative process that inspires them to maximize their personal and professional potential." Where a consultant tends to offer recommendations and answers (advocacy), a coach tends to ask questions and clarify thought processes (inquiry).[4] The part of the Federation's definition that we want to emphasize is the "thought-provoking and creative process," as that reflects the OKRs coaching focus on inquiry.

If you are an experienced coach, making the transition to OKRs coaching may be quite natural. Seasoned coaches often report that they just need to make minor adjustments as they are already asking many of the same questions we classify as "OKRs questions."

However, if you are making the transition from consulting to coaching, you may need to make a concerted effort to focus on inquiry rather than simply giving advice. An OKRs coach does not focus on providing answers; an OKRs coach focuses on clarifying and providing the questions that help their client find their own answers.

Whether you have a consulting or coaching background, it is essential that you balance advice with inquiry. Inquiry is foundational to OKRs coaching and helps discover answers. An OKRs coach must know when to provide advice on the best way to phrase the answers in the context of objectives and key results as well. To arrive at a definition of OKRs coaching, it helps to understand your role as an OKRs coach and the extent to which you advise or inquire at each of the three phases of OKRs coaching.[5] Notice how your role shifts between acting as a consultant in Phase 1, as you advise and guide your client, to being a coach in Phase 3, as you focus on inquiry to let your client create and reflect on their OKRs.

In Phase 1, OKRs deployment coaching, you take a structured approach with your client to align on the answers to the critical questions that will define their OKRs program. During this phase, you play both a coach and consultant role. While you do ask questions, your client often looks to you for guidance about how best to get their OKRs project going. You advise your client based on your knowledge of OKRs best practices and lessons learned from prior OKRs deployments.

Let's define this first phase as *OKRs deployment coaching:* a structured series of discussions in which the OKRs coach guides a client to (1) align on the answers to the critical questions that define their OKRs program and (2) define the roles and resources that will support the program.

In Phase 2, OKRs training, you introduce your client to OKRs theory and get them to apply this theory in an interactive workshop. You begin as more of a consultant when introducing theory. You end as more of a coach, asking OKRs coaching questions that let your client translate theory into the creative process of drafting their OKRs.

Let's define this second phase as *OKRs training:* an interactive workshop designed to create a common understanding of OKRs through examples and collaboration. You provide both an educational presentation and facilitate a workshop to ensure students translate theory into practice through the creative process of drafting their OKRs.

In Phase 3, OKRs cycle coaching, you focus almost exclusively on coaching. You must be careful not to overplay the role of consultant. You are the expert on OKRs, not your client's business strategy. You guide your client to critically reflect on their most important goals through a series of questions that form the foundation of the OKRs approach. This inquiry is an ongoing process that helps your client complete the OKRs cycle.[6] Phase 3 is, from a content point of view, the most important phase as it mines the client's brain to harvest their critical thinking about their business.

Let's define this third phase as *OKRs cycle coaching:* inquiry that enables a client to critically reflect throughout the three steps of an OKRs cycle to (1) align on where and why to focus effort to make measurable improvement, (2) communicate and monitor progress, and (3) document and apply learnings to the next OKRs cycle. Combining the role an OKRs coach plays across these phases leads to the following definition:

> **OKRs coaching:** Partnering with clients in a thought-provoking, creative, and structured process over three phases.
>
> *Phase 1: Deployment coaching* to align on the answers to the questions that define an OKRs program and define the roles and resources that will support the OKRs program.
>
> *Phase 2: Training* to ensure a shared understanding of OKRs.
>
> *Phase 3: Cycle coaching*, inquiry that enables a client to critically reflect throughout the three steps of an OKRs cycle to (1) align on where and why to focus effort to make measurable improvement, (2) communicate and monitor progress, and (3) document and apply learnings to the next OKRs cycle.

Excerpts from Actual OKRs Coaching Sessions

To bring the definition of OKRs coaching to life, here are two excerpts from actual coaching sessions. The first is taken from a remote 1:1 OKRs drafting session from the beginning of Phase 3, cycle coaching. The second excerpt is taken from an in-person training workshop with a large group at the end of Phase 2, training.[7] Each excerpt includes two columns. The right-hand column provides the transcript of what was said. The left-hand column exposes my thought process as a coach, capturing what I thought and felt but did not say along the way.[8]

Excerpt 1: Remote 1:1 Coaching Session with VP of Engineering

Context: The CEO of a large software company based in the United Kingdom set a top-level goal to be more "sales-driven." Shortly thereafter, I was asked to facilitate a 1:1 remote coaching session to help the VP of engineering, Rajeev, draft OKRs for his team. Rajeev was totally new to OKRs but quite motivated to define goals that clearly aligned with the CEO's top-level vision. This excerpt is taken directly from the transcript of my actual 1:1 coaching session.

1:1 OKRs Coaching Transcript Excerpt

What I was thinking (LHC)	What we said (RHC)
	VP Engineering/Rajeev: My key objective is to help our sales team achieve their targets.
Hmm. I'm not clear how engineers help the sales team achieve their targets. But this VP might have a way to help drive sales, so let's get to the bottom of what he's trying to achieve. I will stick to the basic framework and ask the *fundamental key result coaching question*.	**OKRs Coach/Ben:** At the end of the quarter, how would we know if engineering helped sales achieve their targets?
	Rajeev: Hmm, that's a good question.
	[Pause]
It is not surprising to me that he cannot answer this question—it's unusual when someone can. That's why I'm here. OK good, I feel useful. However, the pause is going on too long, so I guess it's my turn to talk. Let's try to get a data point of where engineering contributed in the past to see if we have a *baseline*.	**Ben:** OK, can you name a customer who purchased within the last year where engineering clearly contributed to the sales process?
	Rajeev: Actually, no. But that would be very good data to have. It's not so much that we help close deals, it's more like we keep the prospect in the mix.
OK, now we're making progress. As I suspected, engineers are not actually closing deals, but I wonder how they "keep the prospect in the mix."	**Aside:** Rajeev proposed two key results:
	1. *"Provide support for 5 major prospects."*
These two statements are directional, but *not measurable*. We must convert these tasks into measurable KRs. For KR1, I'm not clear what "major prospect" means.	2. *"Develop training for sales team."*
I made up "minor" prospect to understand what defines a major prospect.	**Ben:** Is there a distinction between a major prospect and a minor prospect?
	Rajeev: Not really.
Now I'm really confused. Rajeev is making up words like "major prospect." I better see if Rajeev and the sales team are on the same page to ensure *alignment* across departments. This seems like a case where a metric may need to be jointly defined.	**Ben:** Do you and the VP of sales agree on the definition of a "major prospect"?
	[Pause]
	Continued

1:1 OKRs Coaching Transcript Excerpt *(continued)*

What I was thinking (LHC)	What we said (RHC)
Good. "$100,000 potential" sounds more concrete. I like that Rajeev is proposing we run it by the VP. This could improve alignment across teams.	**Rajeev**: Let's replace "major prospect" with "prospect with $100,000 year-1-revenue potential." Then we can run this definition by the VP of sales.
I still don't know what "sales support" means, so I'm going to confirm metric history as this ensures the KR is ***measurable.***	**Ben**: Have you measured the number of these sales support events in the past?
Aha! This could be a ***baseline metric*** as we lack historical measurement.	**Rajeev**: No.
It's time for the ***Fundamental Task-to-Key Result question*** to uncover the intended outcome and focus on ***results not tasks.***	**Ben**: What is the intended outcome of engineering providing sales support?
	Rajeev: It results in a continued sales process or it kills the deal.
Great! We are now closer to measuring the outcome of "sales support." But "killing the deal" does not seem good.	**Ben**: What if all five sales support calls result in dead deals? Will we have achieved this goal?
	Rajeev: No. The meeting is not really considered a success when we lose the deal for technical reasons. Maybe we should define this as, "provide sales support with no more than three $100k+ prospects deciding to not evaluate our product for technical reasons."
We're getting closer! But it feels negative. As we have no historical data, we cannot set a target for the number of "prospects that decide not to evaluate for technical reasons." I will reframe this key result as a baseline metric that is positive.	**Ben**: We're heading in the right direction, but it is framed negatively. I recommend: obtain a baseline on "technical pass rate." If we meet with ten $100k+ prospects and eight advance without technical objection, the technical pass rate is 80 percent.
	Rajeev: That's perfect.

Draft OKR That Resulted from the Coaching Session with Rajeev

Objective: Measure and improve engineering's support of sales.

Why Now? Leadership wants to create a more sales-driven culture and is asking everyone to find a way to contribute to the sales process.

Key Result: Obtain a baseline metric to reflect technical pass rate metric by end of Q2 with 10 documented outcomes from engineering engagements with the sales team on $100k+ prospects.

Outcome: Rajeev liked the idea of tracking the technical pass rate. After the session, Rajeev agreed to confirm with the VP of sales that technical pass rate was a useful metric to quantify the extent to which engineering contributes to sales. The VP of sales reacted favorably and proceeded to describe the columns in the spreadsheet that would be used to start tracking the technical pass rate. The VP of sales felt that this spreadsheet would help prioritize which types of technical objections to focus on removing.

Coaching Takeaways

When in doubt, go back to fundamental OKRs coaching questions such as:

✔ *Fundamental key result question*: How will we know we've achieved the objective?
✔ *Fundamental task-to-key-result question*: What is the intended outcome of the task?

This excerpt focuses on how the vague notion of "supporting sales" was translated into a key result. It is worth noting that we created another key result that translated the task of "develop training materials for sales team" to the measurable key result, "Increase percentage of account managers in one region certified on product X selling technique from 0 to 60 % by the end of Q2."

Excerpt 2: Group Coaching Session with VP of Accounts Receivable and Database Administrator

Context: An IT team brought me in to help expand the use of OKRs from IT into the "business teams." Mary, the VP of accounts receivable, was asked to attend a brief, 30-minute training on OKRs followed by a two-hour workshop to draft OKRs. At first, Mary was resistant to the idea of setting more goals because her team already tracked tons of metrics. She expressed her skepticism about setting OKRs, "We already have tons of data to track. Adding another system is probably the last thing we should do." The CIO as well as several IT managers and other teams from within the finance department participated in the workshop.

After a short presentation on OKRs, I asked each team to take 45 minutes to draft their OKRs. Mary showed me about 25 metrics with nice charts on a dashboard and had a puzzled look on her face. This coaching excerpt starts right after Mary showed me this dashboard. It is presented in the same two-column format as the first excerpt with Rajeev.

Group OKRs Coaching Transcript Excerpt

What I was thinking (LHC)	What we said (RHC)
I see this a lot. People who track lots of data can benefit with some OKRs coaching. Let's ask a question to help her focus on a single objective.	**OKRs Coach/Ben**: I see you're tracking a lot of metrics. It's great that you have lots of data at your fingertips. But what is the most important area for your team to focus on over the next three months?
What does it mean for AR to be strategic?	**VP Finance/Mary**: I want our team to be more strategic about how we handle AR.
I will stick to the basic OKR coaching framework and ask the *fundamental key result coaching question.*	**Ben**: How would we know your team was more strategic about handling AR by the end of the quarter?
Aha! So, now she has focused on a specific metric and her logic makes sense.	**Mary**: The problem is that once AR gets aged 90 days, it's harder to collect. The big opportunity right now is to reduce the AR that is aged over 60 days.
Let's see if we can get a number to quantify this 60-day key result.	**Ben**: What would be the most amazing reduction for AR aged 60 days that you could imagine this coming quarter?
Hmm. We need the baseline so we can write this as a metric key result "from X to Y." But she does seem to have a good feeling for what would be an amazing outcome. So, I'll ask about the current value of AR>60 days later.	**Mary**: I know we can cut it by 10% since we have a few key accounts in there that are going to pay soon, but 50% would really be amazing.
	Aside: Mary's team decided to create just one objective with a single key result. Mary shared her draft key result: **Reduce AR>60 days by 50%.**
	Enter Sumit, a database administrator.
Sumit is asking a good question! I am guessing total dollars but good to clarify.	**Database Administrator/Sumit**: Do you mean reduce the number of customers that have invoices due past 60 days or the total dollars that are past 60 days due?"
	Continued →

Group OKRs Coaching Transcript Excerpt *(continued)*

What I was thinking (LHC)	What we said (RHC)
This is an improvement, more specific. I am not going to interrupt this conversation. It seems like we're on track for some alignment across teams.	**Mary:** OK, let's adjust the key result to reduce the *total dollars* from our invoices that are 60 days or more past due by 50%.
	Aside: The energy in the room changed; everyone was clearly engaged.
Wow! Sumit is excited to run some reports.	**Sumit:** Would you like help with this key result?
This is a great sign, but hold on, now Mary seems mad.	**Mary:** Yes! I asked for help with this last year and I got this great dashboard, but I don't understand how you can help me reduce the AR by 50%.
I love this! Sumit is like the OKRs coach now and is getting Mary to see the value of focus.	**Sumit:** I can provide a report that lists the top accounts by dollar amount that are aged 30–45 days, 46–60 days, and 60–90 days. Then, we can proactively reach out to the big customers who are possibly headed into this AR bucket and the big-ticket items already aged greater than 60 days.
It's much easier to communicate when there is focus on one thing. The critical thinking inherent in OKRs coaching is enabling Mary and Sumit to collaborate.	**Mary:** OK, really? This is just like the report I asked for about a year ago!
	Sumit: Well, you probably ask for a lot of reports, but now you're only asking for one.

Draft OKR from Coaching Session

Mission: Ensure our customers pay in a timely fashion.

Objective: Strategically reduce dollars not yet paid, stuck in accounts receivable.

Why Now? We already track lots of metrics; however, we cannot focus on everything. Research suggests that once a customer passes 60 days past due, odds of recovering that payment drop significantly. Even worse, we often lose these customers, which can damage ongoing revenue.

Key Result: Reduce total dollars that we have invoiced in the 60 or more days past due category by 50 % (at $24 million as of March 31; we want this down to $12 million by August 30).

Outcome: Sumit listened deeply to a single objective with just one key result. Mary got the data she needed to manage AR more strategically. The company ended up reducing dollars in AR, positively impacting cash flow.

Coaching Takeaways

- ✔ *Cross-team alignment.* Mary took time to define her key result in such a way that others outside her team, such as Sumit, could understand. Encourage teams to present key results to dependent teams for feedback before finalizing.
- ✔ *Less is more.* Defining a small set of OKRs improves communication. People seem to pay more attention when there is less content to absorb.

 NOTES

1. Notable tech companies using OKRs in the early 2010s include LinkedIn, Twitter, and Zynga.
2. Here's the link to the Google Ventures OKRs video that got so many views: https://www.youtube.com/watch?v=mJB83EZtAjc.
3. Kuang's book has sold more than 50,000 copies in China as of August 2021.
4. I am inspired to use the distinction of "advocacy versus inquiry" based on the powerful impressions Chris Argyris made on me as a guest lecturer at Stanford. For the purposes of this book, I am equating the "advice" with "advocacy" and "inquiry" with "questioning." More on advocacy and inquiry comes from the field known as "Action Science." For a brief overview, see: https://actiondesign.com/resources/readings/advocacy-and-inquiry. For an academic treatment, see *Action Science*, Chris Argyris, Robert Putnam, and Diana McLain Smith, Jossey-Bass Management Series.

5. We introduce the phases of an OKRs coaching engagement in this first chapter as context for the definition of OKRs coaching. Your role as OKRs coach varies at each phase. So, to understand what it means to be an OKRs coach, you need a deep understanding of the phases. Chapter 2 provides a summary of these phases. Chapters 3, 4, and 5 include detailed playbooks for each phase.
6. Chapter 2 provides an overview of the three steps of the OKRs cycle. Refer to Chapter 5 for a playbook detailing how to coach your client through each step of the cycle.
7. While we do not include a sample coaching excerpt from Phase 1, deployment coaching, Chapter 3 includes resources that will help you coach your client through this first phase.
8. For more on the left-hand column exercise, see *The Fifth Discipline Fieldbook*, Peter Senge, Charlotte Roberts, Art Kleiner, Richard Ross, and Bryan Smith, Currency Doubleday, pp. 246–252.

CHAPTER 1 EXERCISE 1: **BEGIN WITH "WHY?"**

- **Anyone reading this book:** Why do you want to develop your OKRs coaching skills? Why do you feel OKRs coaching is important? Urgent? Interesting?
- **Internal coaches:** If you are helping your company succeed with OKRs, how will developing OKRs coaching skills benefit your organization? How will these skills benefit you personally?
- **External coaches:** If you are coaching your clients, describe why it's worth your time to develop OKRs coaching skills. Do you have a client right now who's using OKRs that you want to support? Are you looking to develop OKRs coaching skills to expand your offering?

CHAPTER 1 EXERCISE 2: **IMPROVE YOUR OKRs COACHING SKILLS WITH A LEFT-HAND COLUMN REFLECTION**

Record an actual OKRs coaching session. Get permission! Use the left-hand column examples at the end of this chapter as inspiration with four sections:

1. **Context:** Start with a few sentences to set the stage for your session.
2. **Right-hand column:** Transcribe what was said.
3. **Left-hand column:** Write down what you thought but did not say.
4. **Outcome:** Include the OKR that evolved along with any key takeaways.

   Bonus: Send your reflection to me via Ben@OKRs.com for feedback.

The OKRs Coaching Engagement

Phases, Duration, and Roles

By the end of this chapter, you will be able to . . .

■ Create a work plan for an OKRs coaching engagement.
■ State the nine roles of an OKRs project and know their responsibilities.
■ Help your client involve the right people at the right time to support their OKRs program.

THE FIELD OF OKRs coaching was in its infancy in 2013. There were no resources available like the book you are reading now. Without a compass, I turned to my mentors and colleagues for guidance. However, as a first-year coach, I could not find answers to basic questions such as: (1) How do I create a proposal with a detailed work plan for an OKRs coaching engagement? (2) How long should the engagement run? (3) Who needs to be involved to support the program? I put in hundreds of hours developing proposals and detailed work plans. Midway through my second year, I created my first systematic approach for scoping out an OKRs coaching engagement.

I spent the next two years testing and validating my initial approach for creating proposals with detailed work plans. I made major changes based on client feedback. In fact, I overhauled the very foundation of a proposal, my pricing structure. I started by pricing services based on the number of teams requesting coaching. Pricing based on the number of teams works in some cases. However, I learned this approach is not reliable.

Defining teams prior to starting the engagement is like fortune telling. In one case, an enthusiastic CEO signed a pricey contract with me based on his request that 20 teams receive OKRs coaching. This all changed unexpectedly right after our first day of training when the CEO decided to set OKRs at the company level only. This left me wondering how to reduce my fee based on the reduction in scope. When I suggested that we modify the original contract in a debrief call, the CEO insisted that we stick to the original fee schedule. He felt like the OKRs project was a massive success, and this success had nothing to do with the number of teams setting OKRs. Nonetheless, I felt like my fee was excessive. In other cases, my clients asked for coaching only at the company level, but they later requested my support with OKRs across multiple business units. This meant much more work than expected. While the occasional instance of scope creep is reasonable, it was happening all too often.

My clients were in a better position to allocate coaching sessions upon completion of their first training workshop. So, I experimented with basing my fee simply on the number of coaching sessions and training workshops rather than guessing up front about the number of teams to include. It worked! We now advise that all coaches develop a standard coaching package as a starting point. Then, we provide pricing for additional coaching and training beyond the initial project scope upon request. By my fifth year, the approach was ready to scale. I expanded my coaching team and created the OKRs Coach Network to review and refine this approach with OKRs coaches around the world.

This chapter outlines a proven formula for creating your coaching engagement work plan based on trial-and-error learning with hundreds of clients. Use it to scope out the three phases, agree on the duration, and ensure your client has the right stakeholders involved to support and sustain their OKRs program. We begin with a diagram (Figure 2.1) to help visualize the phases and steps of an OKRs coaching engagement.

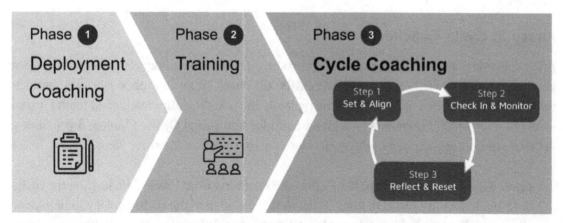

FIGURE 2.1 The three phases of an OKRs coaching engagement

 PHASES IN AN OKRs COACHING ENGAGEMENT

Phase 1: Deployment Coaching

"Which teams will define OKRs?" "How many OKRs will each team set?" "How will we score key results?" Your client's deployment parameters are the answers to these questions and more.[1] While deployment coaching includes defining roles and resources, most of the time is allocated to defining these parameters. OKRs coaching engagements must – let me repeat that, *must* – address deployment parameters. Even when called upon to help an organization with an OKRs program already in place, confirm these parameters with your client, as they are the foundation of any OKRs program. Plan on two to four weeks to define deployment parameters. Chapter 3 provides a detailed analysis of each parameter.

Phase 2: Training

The roles, resources, and parameters defined in Phase 1 inform your client's OKRs training program. Training workshops begin with a brief overview of OKRs and your client's unique deployment parameters. However, dedicate most training time to interactive exercises that get participants applying this theory to develop their OKRs. Here is an OKRs coaching mantra we suggest you internalize: *The best way to learn about OKRs is to get started on your actual OKRs.*[2] Chapter 4 provides a detailed analysis of three distinct training workshops.

Phase 3: Cycle Coaching

After delivering a training workshop to introduce OKRs, you guide your client through a three-step OKRs cycle: (1) set and align OKRs, (2) check in and monitor progress, and (3) reflect and reset. Cycle coaching sessions typically include the entire leadership team for top-level OKRs or several members of a given team for team-level OKRs. Chapter 5 provides a detailed analysis of each step in the cycle. Here's an overview of the three steps.

■ *Cycle Step 1: Set and Align.* While the OKRs training from Phase 2 includes some OKRs drafting, it does not result in final OKRs. In this first step of the OKRs cycle, you help your client set, align, and ultimately publish OKRs in a single location. We call this single location "The OKRs Tracker."

■ *Cycle Step 2: Check In and Monitor.* Publishing OKRs in a single location is a big win. You and your client may be elated at this stage. Creating OKRs often leads to a feeling of increased focus, alignment, and engagement. However, your work is not done. As an effective coach, you ensure your client integrates OKRs into daily work throughout the cycle. Your level of involvement with this step ranges from simply observing a team meeting to facilitating a check-in with multiple teams.

- ***Cycle Step 3: Reflect and Reset.*** When we ask OKRs coaches and our clients what they like most about OKRs, they often reply with a single word, "learning." The three main learning areas are (1) how to optimize the OKRs program, (2) how to better get stuff done at work, and (3) how best to make a business impact. Near the end of the cycle, you facilitate a reflect and reset session to ensure your client applies learnings to the next cycle.

Ongoing Support

Effective OKRs coaches support and guide their clients' OKRs programs even after completing their coaching engagement. At the end of every project, we recommend reviewing each of the three phases with your client. Revisit Phase 1, as deployment parameters are often modified at the end of an OKRs cycle. Revisit Phase 2 to ensure that as new team members adopt OKRs, they have access to OKRs training. As for Phase 3, your client should make cycle coaching available going forward. In fact, we recommend all teams new to OKRs have access to cycle coaching at least for their first cycle.

To maximize the ongoing impact of OKRs, your client should have the internal expertise required to support their OKRs program.[3] However, your client may ask that you return to energize their OKRs program with a keynote presentation or create a video for onboarding new staff.

 DURATION OF AN OKRs COACHING ENGAGEMENT

Structure OKRs coaching engagements for 8 to 12 months. Our default program runs eight months. However, some of our clients prefer to begin with a full year commitment. Either way, build in time for two complete cycles as shown in the sample coaching engagement plan in Figure 2.2.

Your client may ask for an OKRs training workshop or just a few coaching sessions to help them launch their OKRs program. While it can be tempting to provide a single workshop or just a few coaching sessions, explain that OKRs coaching programs work best when there is a structured coaching relationship that runs 8 to 12 months. Here's how we arrived at this conclusion.

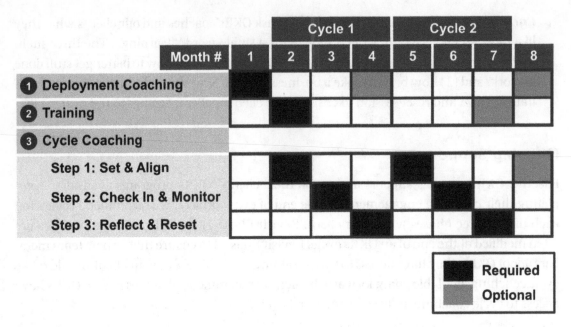

FIGURE 2.2　Sample eight-month OKRs coaching engagement plan with two quarterly cycles

At first, we offered a three-month coaching package. Intuitively, this seemed like the right amount of time to coach a client through a full OKRs cycle. After all, there are three months in a quarter, and the quarterly cycle is the default duration. In this approach, we were always successful delivering an OKRs training workshop based on our client's unique deployment parameters. As well, our clients were happy with the OKRs that they published upon completing step 1 of the OKRs cycle. However, some of these early OKRs projects were not successful.

While nearly everyone left our workshops excited about OKRs, many did not integrate OKRs into their daily work throughout the quarter. Even worse, the three-month program did not always allow time to close the loop with each team to capture learnings and apply them to the next OKRs cycle.

To build in time for this reflection, we expanded to a four-month program. This extra month ensured we had time before and after the OKRs cycle to prep and debrief. We saw an immediate improvement. We coached every client throughout an entire OKRs cycle. However, after a year or so, we realized even four months was not enough time. We discovered that supporting clients through two cycles works best.

A typical two-cycle OKRs coaching program runs eight months. This model works; we use it with great success. The first cycle emphasizes learning, not scale. It focuses on a pilot group rather than the entire organization. In the second cycle, you apply learnings to explore how best to expand. Your client may want to move quickly to roll out OKRs across their entire organization; however, rather than making the leap from crawl to run, we find a *crawl-walk-run* approach works best. This is your next OKRs coaching mantra: Take a *crawl-walk-run* approach when rolling out OKRs.

Crawl-walk-run reflects our general guidance to begin with a smaller set of pilot teams and get OKRs right before scaling the use of OKRs to the larger organization. When we advise our clients to "walk before you run," they agree it is best to slow down. Our clients typically hold off on scaling their OKRs programs until the third or fourth cycle.

Most of our clients reach out to touch base from time to time after completing their second OKRs cycle. However, rather than waiting for your client to reach out after completing your OKRs engagement, we suggest proactively checking in with your client contact every month or two. This contact is often the OKRs project lead, one of the key roles in an OKRs coaching engagement.

 ## ROLES IN AN OKRs COACHING ENGAGEMENT

Agreeing on the roles required to support the OKRs program and who will fill each role is critical to your client's success. One OKRs coach reviewing early drafts of this book, Omid Akhavan, suggested that we include definitions of these roles and responsibilities in one place. So, Omid and fellow OKRs coaches, this section is for you.

In addition to clarifying your role as external OKRs coach, ensure that your client understands each of the roles in Figure 2.3. We recommend taking time to identify who will fill certain roles even before inking a coaching agreement. While you need not fill every role right away, all roles should be filled by the time you complete the first OKRs cycle.

Role	Key Responsibilities	When to Define
1. External OKRs Coach	Coach client through three phases	Proposal
2. Executive Sponsor	Bring energy and life to the program	Proposal
3. OKRs Project Lead	Primary contact for external coach	Proposal
4. OKRs Coordinator	Schedule coaching sessions	Phase 1, first call
5. HR Lead	Ensure OKRs do not conflict with performance management	Phase 1, first call
6. Team Lead	Support OKRs cycle within their team	Prior to Phase 2
7. Team Member	Help draft team-level OKRs	Prior to Phase 3
8. Key Result Champion	Serve as point person for KR progress	Phase 3, Step 1
9. Internal OKRs Coach	Provide ongoing coaching support	Near end of Phase 3

FIGURE 2.3   The nine roles in an OKRs coaching engagement

1. External OKRs Coach

This is you. As an external OKRs coach, you help your client successfully deploy OKRs. Unlike a trainer who might lead a day or two of focused training and then head back home, external coaches plan on longer-term relationships. We advise applying the approach outlined in this book to ensure your clients complete two OKRs cycles. With cycle times typically set for three to four months, OKRs coaching engagements that include helping your client align on their deployment parameters, complete training workshops, and two OKRs cycles tend to run 8 to 12 months.

Responsibilities of external OKRs coaches include:[4]

- **Deployment coaching.** Facilitate definitions of deployment parameters and align on the roles and resources to support the OKRs program.
- **Training.** Lead training workshops to create a shared understanding of OKRs.
- **Cycle coaching.** Ensure completion of OKRs cycle and capture learnings to apply to the next cycle.

2. Executive Sponsor

This is the most senior person in the organization that is supporting the OKRs program. In small companies, the executive sponsor is often the CEO. In larger companies, the sponsor is often the leader of a department, region, or business unit implementing OKRs.

Executive sponsors review and approve the deployment parameters that define their OKRs program. Once approved, the parameters can be used to inform the creation of OKRs FAQs and training materials. In addition to approving deployment parameters, the executive sponsor helps shape the development of top-level OKRs. As with any change management program, an OKRs program will have almost no chance of success without executive support. The executive sponsor must clearly state why the organization is adopting OKRs and incorporate OKRs into leadership presentations and management meetings.

Responsibilities of executive sponsors include:

- Communicate why the organization is adopting OKRs.
- Confirm deployment parameters as recommended by project leads.
- Help gather objectives for the top-level OKRs drafting workshop.
- Participate in top-level OKRs workshops.
- Meet with team leads to confirm team-level OKRs are aligned with the organization's strategy.
- Bring energy and life to the OKRs program (e.g., secure resources, make opening remarks at OKRs trainings, present top-level OKRs at companywide meetings).

3. OKRs Project Lead

At organizations with fewer than 100 employees, the CEO or COO often takes on the OKRs project lead role when getting started. In larger companies, this role is well suited for mid-level managers. An OKRs project lead must be a great communicator and possess general knowledge of his or her organization's structure and business model. This role can require a serious commitment for the first month or two when the focus is on deployment parameters and training workshops. However, the OKRs project lead role is generally not a full-time job. Rather, it is one of three to five key responsibilities. Once the OKRs program is up and running, an OKRs project lead should plan for four to eight hours a week near the beginning and end of each OKRs cycle but just an hour or two per week during the middle of the cycle. Executive assistants, chiefs of staff, and agile coaches often make excellent OKRs project leads.

We recommend two OKRs project leads. In cases where there is just one person in this role, that one person may become dependent on the external coach or grow frustrated that they do not have an in-house colleague to help optimize the program. While two project leads are better than one, the incremental value of adding a third may not justify the cost.[5]

When a prospective client approaches you to explore OKRs coaching support, expect the person (or people) reaching out to take on the OKRs project lead role. While the CEO may play this role to help get the OKRs program off the ground, be sure your client identifies a mid-level manager to become an OKRs project lead as well. A CEO is a great asset as an OKRs project lead, but it can be problematic if he or she is the only one. CEOs are often hard to track down and are notorious for canceling meetings at the last minute.

Responsibilities of OKRs project leads include:

- Attend all deployment coaching sessions.
- Present recommendations to leadership (e.g., how to score key results).
- Work with external OKRs coach to agree on an OKRs tracker tool.
- Attend some, but not all, OKRs cycle coaching sessions.
- Facilitate OKRs training workshops (e.g., send workshop invites and compile objectives to be used at training workshops).
- Coordinate and schedule OKRs coaching sessions.*

4. OKRs Coordinator

We added an asterisk next to the last item, "coordinate and schedule OKRs coaching sessions," because OKRs project leads often delegate this responsibility to another person. This other person is quite likely the "OKRs coordinator." Some organizations have a single person play both the role of OKRs project lead and OKRs coordinator. However, the roles and required skill sets are quite different.

Think of the OKRs coordinator as a task master. OKRs coordinators help keep the program on track. They seek to ensure people are engaged and have access to the information they need to succeed with OKRs. While we recommend two project leads, we recommend a single person play the role of OKRs coordinator.

The coordinator sends reminders to ensure teams complete each step in the OKRs cycle. For example, they may send a reminder email asking team leads to send draft OKRs to the external coach prior to their coaching session. They may send emails to remind team leads to set up reflect and reset sessions two weeks prior to the upcoming OKRs cycle. They often schedule coaching sessions with the external OKRs coach. The OKRs coordinator may be charged with asking each team to submit learnings from their reflect and reset sessions at the end of each cycle.

Responsibilities of OKRs coordinators include:

- Coordinate and schedule OKRs coaching sessions.
- Send email reminders to ensure OKRs cycle stays on track such as:
  Step 1: Send email a week or two into the cycle with a link to the OKRs tracker to ensure everyone posts their OKRs to a single location by a target date.
  Step 2: Send email reminders to identify key results to be shared at mid-cycle check-ins.
  Step 3: Remind each team to publish their learnings at the end of the OKRs cycle.

5. Human Resources Lead

About half of our clients proactively include someone from HR from the start. Often, this HR person is also an OKRs project lead. While involvement from HR is important, at least one OKRs project lead should not be from HR. If all OKRs project leads are from HR, the program is at risk of becoming an "HR thing." OKRs should not be experienced as a program that is forced on an organization by a single department.

Although OKRs projects can fail due to being led by HR, they can also fail when HR is left out entirely. It is critical that the HR lead participates in at least one deployment coaching session to align on how OKRs relate to performance management.[6]

Responsibilities of HR leads include:

- Provide input to help define deployment parameters.
- Assess how to relate OKRs with performance management.
- Involve project leads outside of HR to ensure OKRs does not become "an HR thing."

6. Team Lead

When helping your client define OKRs at the team level, you and your client must agree on a list of teams setting OKRs, along with who is leading each team. By default, when using the org chart to define teams for OKRs, team leads become the persons at the top of the hierarchy. If this is the case, be sure to get a copy of your client's org chart.[7]

Responsibilities of team leads include:

- Participate in OKRs training.
- Facilitate OKRs development with their team.
- Complete an OKRs cycle; attend cycle coaching sessions.
- Document and apply learnings to next cycle.

7. Team Member

Team members comprise everyone other than the team lead on a given team setting OKRs. Team members work together to impact key results. OKRs are most effective when team members participate in the creation of OKRs. While team leads tend to define most objectives, team members participate actively in OKRs drafting sessions and help to define most key results.

Team members apply critical thinking to continuously connect their work to the bigger picture, often through one-on-ones with their manager. They know how their work helps impact OKRs and/or contributes to keeping health metrics on track.

Responsibilities of team members include:

- Participate in drafting team-level OKRs.
- Help refine key results at the team level, especially when aligning on prescoring (i.e., stretch, target, or commit).[8]
- Apply OKRs critical thinking to connect work to the bigger picture.

8. Key Result Champion

A key result must have a name next to it. We call this name the key result champion. Each organization defines this role slightly differently. Some organizations insist on having a single champion to ensure accountability. Others prefer to add a second champion when key results are highly dependent to balance accountability with alignment and collaboration.

Nearly half of our clients require two champions for each key result. For example, some require an executive sponsor and a mid-level champion to ensure vertical alignment. The executive sponsor does not manage the key result on a day-to-day basis. Instead, the executive sponsor is expected to update the CEO on the status of the key result at leadership meetings. One of our clients wanted to ensure boundary-spanning alignment to ensure that OKRs reduced silo effects. Therefore, each key result had a primary champion within the team setting the OKR as well as a horizontal partner, a co-champion from a highly dependent team, who had their name listed next to the key result as well. It is unusual for our clients to assign three or more names to a key result. They find adding a third name reduces accountability.[9]

How your client selects team members to fill this role should reflect the reason why they've chosen to deploy OKRs in the first place. If accountability is the primary motivation for deploying OKRs, a single name for each key result may be best. If OKRs are intended to increase alignment across teams, two names may work best. Some organizations do not embrace the term *champion* and prefer *key result manager* or *key result lead*. That's fine. However, we do not recommend the term *key result owner*.[10]

Responsibilities of key result champions include:

- Update progress and confidence scores throughout the cycle.
- Serve as point person for questions related to the key result.
- Welcome ideas for how best to move the key result forward.
- Communicate and ensure alignment on work related to the key result. For example, ensure teams do not perform redundant tasks or work on conflicting projects.
- Apply learnings from the key result to the next cycle. Whether or not the key result is achieved, champions communicate final scores, assess impact, capture learnings, and recommend whether to keep, modify, or remove key results.

9. Internal OKRs Coach

An internal OKRs coach plays a role nearly identical to that of an external coach. Unlike external coaches, internal OKRs coaches are employees of the company deploying OKRs and have job responsibilities beyond supporting OKRs. While external OKRs coaches bring OKRs expertise and an outside perspective, internal coaches also bring unique value. They often know the history, business model, and inner workings of their organization.

Organizations that use OKRs effectively tend to have at least one internal OKRs coach for every 50 employees that are included in their OKRs program. So, a company with 500 employees involved with OKRs should plan on at least 10 internal OKRs coaches to support their OKRs project. In our experience, the more internal coaches, the better. In fact, one of our clients has an engineering capabilities team with an especially high level of in-house OKRs expertise. They have about one internal OKRs coach for every three team members. This engineering capability team's OKRs process at each step in the cycle is beautiful to observe. Agile coaches, SCRUM masters, and HR business partners often make excellent internal OKRs coaches.

Responsibilities of internal OKRs coaches include:

- Attend OKRs training sessions.
- Ensure their team completes the OKRs cycle by asking questions to help refine OKRs, prepping for the mid-cycle check-in, and facilitating reflect and reset sessions at the end of each cycle.
- Lead workshops to train other internal OKRs coaches.

Is an External Coach Required?

Some organizations deploy OKRs successfully with internal resources only. However, in our experience, organizations consistently report that engaging an external coach is a high-value proposition. An outside expert provides unbiased feedback based on best practices. This feedback improves the quality of OKRs across the organization. In addition, OKRs project leads find external OKRs coaches help keep the OKRs project on track. Executive teams often report that the very presence of an external coach adds value, keeping the executive team respectful of one another and focused on OKRs as a critical thinking framework.[11]

Coaching Takeaways

- ✔ Structure OKRs engagements to support your client through two cycles (8–12 months).
- ✔ Create work plans based on the phases in an OKRs coaching engagement: (1) deployment coaching, (2) training, and (3) cycle coaching.
- ✔ Help your client identify the right people to play the various roles required to launch and sustain their OKRs program.
- ✔ To ensure an OKRs program is not viewed as "an HR thing," include at least one OKRs project lead outside of the HR function.

NOTES

1. Most of our clients are fine with the term *deployment parameters*. However, some prefer using different words such as *rules of the road, guardrails,* or *FAQs*. Use whatever terminology works best for your client.

2. Here is how we arrived at this OKRs coaching mantra, which simplifies to: *the only way to learn OKRs is to do OKRs*. Early clients demanded more examples of OKRs related to their specific industry or situation. However, after adding these examples, our clients complained that our workshops had too many examples. We learned that our clients did not want to see our examples. They wanted to see *their* OKRs! We now present very few examples of OKRs. Our clients begin drafting their own OKRs as soon as possible in training workshops.

3. Organizations that have a trained group of internal OKRs coaches are better positioned for the long term. Refer to the expert training application in Chapter 4 for details.

4. Review the definition of OKRs coaching in Chapter 1 as inspiration to help you reflect on your role as OKRs coach. We recommend reviewing your role with each client to confirm that it matches their expectations.

5. It is sometimes best to define more than three project leads. For example, if your client has several regions or business units deploying OKRs, we recommend including one to two project leads from each region or business unit.

6. The issue of OKRs and performance management can be a hot topic for certain organizations. In such cases, we recommend that you confirm their recommended approach with an executive sponsor from the start. Refer to the seventh deployment parameter in Chapter 3 for more on how to relate OKRs to performance.

7. See the first deployment parameter in Chapter 3 for an analysis of why using the org chart to define OKRs teams may not be optimal.

8. Refer to the third deployment parameter in Chapter 3 for an analysis of prescoring key results to align on various levels of achievement such as commit, target, and stretch.

9. While unusual, one of our clients requires three champions per key result. They have large squads and find it best to include a champion from (1) program management, (2) product management, and (3) engineering.

10. Our clients once added a name next to each key result and referred to this person as the *key result owner*. However, this term is no longer in use. No team-level key result should be considered a single person's job.

11. A recent client let us know, "Having Ben and Dikran as our external coaches was like having 'tough parents.' It was exactly what we needed to get on the right path with OKRs."

12. Work plans and sample proposals are available to members of the OKRs Coaching Network.

CHAPTER 2 EXERCISE 1: **CREATE A WORK PLAN**

- Include the three phases with a rough timeline.
- Use the sample plan from Figure 2.2 as inspiration.[12]

CHAPTER 2 EXERCISE 2: **IDENTIFY AND STAFF ROLES**

Reflect on the process of defining and staffing the roles to support an OKRs deployment.

- Were you an external or internal coach?
- How many OKRs project leads were involved?
- How well do you feel each role was defined?
- How well did each person perform his or her role? What could be better?

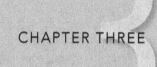

CHAPTER THREE

Playbook for
Phase 1 – Deployment Coaching

By the end of this chapter, you will be able to . . .

- Explain why OKRs coaching begins with deployment parameters.
- Help your client define 10 universal deployment parameters.
- Identify other parameters to capture client nuances.

N 2015, I FLEW to Paris to facilitate an OKRs training workshop. My client requested that I spend a full day with their leadership team to introduce OKRs. So, I took the project and did exactly what I was hired to do. At the time, I was still figuring out my approach. I did not know about the three phases outlined in Chapter 2. I was not clear about how best to prepare for the workshop. My client suggested we have a couple calls prior to the workshop to align on the agenda. After these two brief calls, I packed my bags and headed to the airport.

The workshop in Paris did not go so well. Although we eventually drafted some decent OKRs, we spent most of the afternoon debating how to deploy OKRs. I was bombarded with questions like (1) "How will these OKRs work with our current system of KPIs?" (2) "I read that OKRs should be decoupled from performance reviews, but how is that possible given they represent our most important goals?" and (3) "If top-level key results do not become team-level objectives like John Doerr's football team example, how can we ensure alignment?"[1]

I had plenty of time to reflect on that training workshop in Paris. I spent the 12-hour flight home writing in my journal, uncovering the critical questions that must be answered prior to an OKRs training workshop. I named the answers to these questions *deployment parameters*. Your client's deployment parameters are the foundation for their OKRs program. Your client uses these parameters to communicate how they are deploying OKRs to the entire organization.

There is no one-size-fits-all, definitive list of deployment parameters; however, we recommend covering 10 parameters with every client. Therefore, we refer to these parameters as "universal." Aligning on the 10 universal parameters with your client prior to delivering a training workshop is always time well spent.

This chapter provides a detailed analysis of the 10 universal deployment parameters and concludes with a sample list of other deployment parameters that you may find important to cover with certain clients.[2] To create context for aligning on these parameters, begin by confirming why your client wants to leverage OKRs.

BEGIN WITH "WHY?"

Most workers are busier than ever, and therefore, to cut through the noise and get a commitment to OKRs, your client's leadership team must be able to provide a compelling answer to why they are implementing OKRs and how employees will benefit. As for the answer itself, each organization should provide a unique response. Bad answers come in two flavors:

1. *Imitation.* "We're implementing OKRs because Google does it," or "We read *Measure What Matters* and lots of successful companies are using it, so we will, too."
2. *Too broad.* "We're implementing OKRs to improve focus, alignment, execution, accountability, transparency, engagement, clarity, continuous improvement, and organizational learning, as well as shifting our mindset from output to outcomes." Listing too many buzzwords when explaining "Why OKRs?" dilutes the message.

Good answers explain the specific problem that leadership seeks to solve by introducing OKRs. Some examples taken directly from CEOs explaining why they've decided to deploy OKRs, followed by a brief analysis of how their answer informs the selection of deployment parameters are:

Cross-Functional Alignment

CEO on "Why OKRs?" "We've doubled in size over the last year. As we scale, we are seeing silo effects typical of larger corporations. To preserve our collaborative culture, we are introducing OKRs. We believe the common goal language of OKRs can prevent these silo effects, improving alignment and communication across teams."

Impact on Deployment. Consider starting with company-level OKRs only. Have each team explore how they can work together to achieve higher-level goals.

Focus

CEO on "Why OKRs?" "We have too much on our plates. There are endless potential projects to take on. However, if we try to take on more over the next few years, we risk failing in many areas rather than succeeding in our core growth areas. We're bringing in OKRs to help us focus on what matters most."

Impact on Deployment. Consider defining a single OKR for each team. It is not the goal for teams to include all their work in this OKR. Simply define one focus area for near-term improvement.

Better Communicate Company Strategy

CEO on "Why OKRs?" "As a leadership team, we feel we have a well-defined strategy. However, we keep getting feedback from our staff that they do not even know we have a strategy. We need to better articulate our strategy and ensure leadership clearly presents the strategy at quarterly updates. We are adopting OKRs to communicate our company's strategy in a consistent format."

Impact on Deployment. Start with company-level OKRs only. Communicate OKRs at recurring meetings, such as a quarterly all-hands.

In practice, it is quite rare to ask your client, "Why OKRs?" and get a concise answer. Ask this question several times and get input from multiple sources. Leadership's answer to this question will be most critical, but test to see that leadership's motivation for deploying OKRs resonates with OKRs project leads, team leads, and team members.[3] Your client's motivation for deploying OKRs informs their selection of deployment parameters.

Coaching Takeaways

✔ Interview executives and OKRs project leads to confirm why your client is implementing OKRs.

✔ The more clarity you and your client have about why they are rolling out OKRs, the easier it will be to align on deployment parameters.

TEN UNIVERSAL DEPLOYMENT PARAMETERS

1. At What Level Will We Set OKRs?

This parameter explores if, how, and when to define OKRs at various levels in an organization. These levels include top/company, team, and individual. Rather than rolling out OKRs at multiple levels all at once, we suggest introducing various levels over time. For example, you may choose to begin with top-level OKRs only and plan to introduce team-level OKRs after succeeding at the top level. As you read through this section, notice that how you define "top/company level" as well as "team level" is not quite as obvious as it might seem at first.

Top/Company Level

We advise beginning OKRs coaching engagements with a mindset that your client will benefit by defining OKRs at the company level. OKRs at higher levels create context for OKRs at lower levels in the organization. To set OKRs at the company level, you must interface directly with the CEO. Assuming you have access to the CEO and can confirm that your client wants to define OKRs for the overall company, the company-level OKRs become the top-level OKRs. However, defining OKRs at the company level is not always the right place to start.

Your client may define a set of top-level OKRs that exist below the company level. There are two reasons for this: (1) feasibility and (2) effectiveness. Feasibility is obvious: You may not have access to the CEO, especially in large companies with thousands of employees. The second reason is less obvious: Company-level OKRs may not be effective. That is, the process of defining company-level OKRs may not be of value. Many of our clients in the Global 1000 with hundreds of products and departments already have a strategic planning system in place that obviates the need for company-level OKRs. In these massive organizations, introducing OKRs at a lower level often makes more sense.

Our clients have defined the top level as the office of the CIO, a business unit, and even a single product team. One of our larger clients with dozens of business units chose to define top-level OKRs for each business unit. The company maintains an annual budget and metrics dashboard to capture the financials of each business unit and felt it would be a redundant exercise to define OKRs for the overall company.

Team Level

We recommend getting top-level OKRs right before rolling out OKRs to lower-level teams. This enables leaders to lead by example and may provide the context teams need to connect their OKRs to top-level goals. If your client is eager to roll out OKRs across teams on day one, advise them to pilot OKRs with several teams prior to scaling their program. How your client chooses to implement OKRs at the team level is a critical predictor of their success with OKRs.

Your client's definition of *team* can make or break their OKRs program. When I worked at Betterworks, the leading OKRs software solution in 2013, we started every implementation by loading the org chart into our software. This automated the process of defining OKRs teams. Oh, wouldn't it be nice if we could simply define teams based on a one-to-one mapping to the org chart? While the org chart approach is simple and scalable, we find it is not always effective. In fact, we have encountered very few cases in which the org chart approach is effective across an entire organization over the long haul.

Dozens of organizations have approached us for coaching and guidance after concluding that their org chart approach failed. One of the most common complaints is that a functional team approach increased silo effects rather than alignment across teams. Defining team-level OKRs based solely on the org chart often conflicts with the "work together" part of the definition of OKRs.

While no single approach works with every organization to define an optimal set of teams that should set OKRs, there are several approaches to consider based on what is proven to work in the field. Here are the three most common ways we've seen organizations think beyond their org charts to set up team-level OKRs that encourage cross-functional alignment. As you review each of the three approaches, keep in mind that they are not mutually exclusive. For example, your client might merge highly dependent teams, case 1, as well as define a cross-functional team based on a top-level OKR, case 3.

Case 1: Merge Highly Dependent Teams   In an OKRs engagement with a mid-sized tech company, an engineering manager asked, "Do we set up separate OKRs for the product team and a separate set of OKRs for the engineering team?" I replied with, "Given you have a separate head of product and head of engineering, then yes, we should define one set of OKRs for the product team and another for engineering." In other words, I was sticking to the assumption that the org chart structure defines OKRs teams. But this was not the right answer. After a few minutes attempting to draft OKRs with just the product team, we concluded that nearly every key result was dependent on engineering. As my client's motivation for implementing OKRs was to increase alignment across teams, we immediately adjusted the game plan to ensure we did not reinforce silo effects by strictly adhering to the org chart.

In the spirit of keeping things simple, we merged product and engineering into a single OKRs team and named this team "ProdEng." In the next cycle, we identified critical dependencies with marketing, so we expanded the team to include a few members from marketing. As this OKRs team loosened the constraint of defining their OKRs based purely on the org chart, we took a step toward creating more alignment across teams. We adjusted the default approach of using the org chart to define teams and leveraged OKRs as a common framework for aligning on a smaller number of OKRs that were shared across the org chart.

Given the reality that product and engineering were still functional teams and had their own cadence and sprint cycles, we agreed to identify a key result champion from the product team and co-champion from engineering for each key result. Simply developing OKRs that spanned the org chart and included the right people from the start improved alignment. This same approach often works with sales and marketing, IT and finance, or any other collection of highly dependent teams.

Case 2: Leverage Existing Cross-Functional Squads From 2014 to 2017, I was lucky enough to coach several leading online classified companies using OKRs in the United States, Canada, and the Netherlands. The online classified company in Canada completely abandoned the notion of functional team OKRs. They had an org chart with a clearly defined reporting structure. However, the org chart was totally decoupled from the teams that set OKRs.

Rather than a list of OKRs teams based on the org chart (e.g., product, engineering, human resources, finance, sales), the teams that set OKRs were mapped to the needs of various customer segments. This mapping reflected their cultural focus on customer centricity. Team-level OKRs were associated with cross-functional squads, each named after their customer segment. They included "Buyer Squad," "Seller Squad," "Auto Squad," "Advertiser Squad," as shown in Figure 3.1.

FUNCTIONAL TEAMS Defined by org chart	CROSS-FUNCTIONAL SQUADS Not defined by org chart
Product	**Buyer Squad**
Engineering	**Seller Squad**
Human Resources	**Auto Squad**
Finance	**Advertiser Squad**
Sales	
Marketing	

FIGURE 3.1 Two common ways to define OKRs teams

Figure 3.1 lists four squads defined by customer segments. However, this is just one example. One of our clients, a leading global e-commerce company, defines squads based on different parts of their customer's journey. Its customer journey squads include: "Account Registration," "Checkout," "Payment and Fraud," "Last Mile Delivery," and "Recommendations."

In his book *Inspired*, Marty Cagan describes a squad as a best-practice approach for designing product teams:

> A product team is a cross-functional set of professionals, typically comprised of a product manager, a product designer, and a small number of engineers. In addition, there are sometimes additional people with specialized skills included on the team such as a data analyst, a user researcher, or a test automation engineer. . . . The key is that these people with their different skill sets usually come from different functional departments in the company, but they sit and work all day, everyday. . . . It's not unusual in larger organizations to have on the order of 20 to 50 of these cross-functional product teams, each responsible for different areas, and each product team with its own objectives to work on.[4]

In 2017, we started seeing more and more organizations, especially in high tech, move beyond the org chart to define their OKRs based on cross-functional squads. Leading organizations such as eBay, PayPal, Nike, and Walmart have implemented product squads. When such squads are in place, organizations find it intuitive to define OKRs at the team level for each cross-functional squad.

Case 3: Define Cross-Functional Teams Based on Top-Level OKRs Our clients mentioned in case 2 defined cross-functional squads prior to launching OKRs. In such cases, we advise defining team-level OKRs based on existing squads. However, many organizations do not have such cross-functional squads in place. Identifying potential cross-functional squads is an unexpected benefit of the OKRs process.

Starting with top-level OKRs may lead to the formation of OKRs teams that go beyond the org chart. One of our clients did just this. After facilitating a training workshop with key leaders, we created a top-level objective focused on organic growth. The CFO pointed out that the five-year financial model depended on maintaining an organic growth rate of at least 50%. However, there was no team responsible for monitoring and maintaining organic growth. Rather than asking each functional team to define OKRs in the context of top-level objectives, our client decided to create a new team focused on organic growth. This team included leaders from several functional areas and was charged with defining and managing the company's organic growth objective.

Individual Level

If your client wants to set individual-level OKRs, we advise making this practice optional. Other than Google, we have not seen an organization succeed when mandating individual-level OKRs for all employees. Some organizations force individuals to define their OKRs by a certain date and load them into a certain location as a compliance ritual. Such practices introduce overhead and often create unintended consequences. Here's an anonymous story from a former customer success manager of an OKRs software vendor that illustrates some of these consequences.

> One of our clients was an irate inbound call center manager. Her company had recently purchased OKRs software licenses for every employee and instructed all staff to publish their OKRs into the software tool by a certain date. She asked me how a given person working in the call center could possibly benefit by loading their personal goals into an OKRs software tool given that she already installed a call-center tracking system that monitored every metric. She claimed, "No one at our company other than me cares about the individual performance of the workers in our call center." Call center employees already had a real-time dashboard that

measured every metric that could possibly be worth tracking. The tracking tool cost quite a bit and was running well. We agreed with the call center manager that it would actually be a step backward if each of the nearly 200 call center workers were forced to copy and paste their metrics and load them into our software tool as a compliance exercise.

—Anonymous OKRs software customer success manager

We recommend that your client explore individual-level OKRs only after succeeding with team-level OKRs for at least two cycles. Even then, we advise organizations not to require that all employees define individual-level OKRs, as this often turns an OKRs program into yet another compliance exercise. When individuals set OKRs for themselves, they often worry, rightfully so, that the achievement of OKRs will be used to evaluate their performance. As such, rather than setting stretch goals, they define key results with low targets so they can underpromise and overdeliver.

Yes, Google has thousands of employees setting OKRs at the individual level. While this approach has worked well for some workers at Google, we've spoken with Googlers who report that individual-level OKRs are a waste of their time. In extreme cases, individual-level OKRs become personal goals that are totally disconnected from business goals.[5]

We've met with a few teams at Twitter who abandoned the practice of setting OKRs at the individual level. These teams stopped setting individual-level OKRs for two reasons. First, most OKRs at the individual level looked like a list of key tasks rather than key results. Second, some teams failed to make progress on team-level OKRs, even though most individual-level OKRs were achieved. In this case, the practice of defining individual-level OKRs led to unintended consequences. Individual contributors tended to focus more on individual-level OKRs rather than working as a team to achieve higher-level OKRs.[6] So, if individuals do not define their own OKRs, how do individuals connect their work to OKRs? How do individual contributors stay engaged?

Individual contributors can – and should – be actively engaged with OKRs at higher levels. Some individuals engage with OKRs by taking on roles such as team member, internal OKRs coach, and/or key result champion. Individuals often discuss OKRs during their regular 1:1s with their manager. Some use OKRs as context for focusing their effort on activities that drive OKRs forward. However, as OKRs do not capture all work, individuals also allocate their time to business-as-usual activities that maintain health metrics (e.g., update software to ensure website uptime remains >99.99%) or are simply required for compliance (e.g., provide reports to support the auditors).[7]

The guidance to begin with top-level OKRs and to avoid requiring individual-level OKRs is universal. However, your approach to choosing the teams that will set OKRs is perhaps the most important deployment parameter of all. This is an opportunity for your client to translate their corporate culture into the fabric of their OKRs program. Let's summarize three cases:

1. ***You want a hierarchical culture.*** Maybe you will choose the default approach to define OKRs teams based on the functional teams in the org chart. In this case, OKRs can help reinforce the org chart hierarchy.
2. ***You want a culture that fosters cross-functional execution.*** Consider merging highly dependent functional teams to build your OKRs teams. This approach embraces dependencies and meets them head on. You may also define top-level OKRs first and see if teams emerge as illustrated in case 3 in which our client created a cross-functional squad to manage organic growth.
3. ***You want a customer-centric culture.*** Consider defining team-level OKRs based on the cross-functional squad model as illustrated in case 2. Leverage this approach with clients that already have squads in place.

Coaching Takeaways

- ✔ Begin by identifying your client's top-level OKRs as context for lower levels.
- ✔ Advise your client to first succeed with a small group of pilot teams before scaling their OKRs program.
- ✔ If your client defines OKRs at the individual level, advise them to make this practice optional.
- ✔ Individual contributors engage with OKRs by taking on roles such as team member, internal OKRs coach, and key result champion.
- ✔ Managers should work with each team member to ensure that daily work activities support moving OKRs forward and/or maintaining health metrics.

2. How Many OKRs Will We Set? Will We Include an Internal Objective?

Back in the 1980s, most teams set five to seven objectives, each with three to five key results. Now, in the 2020s, we find it unusual for a team to set more than three objectives. The fact that teams are defining a smaller set of OKRs is probably a good thing. After all, OKRs are intended to increase focus. As OKRs coaches, we live by the mantra *less is more*.

We advise limiting OKRs to a narrow area of focus rather than attempting to map all work to OKRs. In general, we advise teams to define at most three objectives and four key results per objective. The optimal number of OKRs varies from team to team, so don't be too rigid about the number of OKRs.[8] Given that OKRs should not attempt to capture all work, most of our clients require any teams that are setting OKRs to focus on at most three objectives that capture 40% to 80% of their total work effort.[9] Although we advise adhering to the *less is more* mantra, certain teams may benefit from another approach.

Some teams capture more than 90% of their work effort in their OKRs. This can work well for resource-constrained teams that serve multiple stakeholders and are constantly inundated with requests to take on new projects. These teams use OKRs as a shield to protect their team members from getting pulled into new directions in the middle of the OKRs cycle. They use OKRs to send the message, "If you don't see it in our OKRs, we're not working on it right now." These teams tend to define as many as five objectives, each with as many as five key results. While we do not advise teams attempt to capture 90% of their work in their OKRs, we recognize this approach may work for teams looking to adopt OKRs as a way of communicating what they are not prioritizing. In our experience, engineering, platform, and infrastructure teams may benefit from this approach.

On the other extreme, some OKRs experts recommend teams align on a single objective.[10] As of 2020, we find that most teams we coach prefer to focus on a single OKR during their learning cycle. Then, after succeeding with one OKR, they explore multiple OKRs in their next cycle. In general, we advise that teams just starting out with OKRs aim for just one or two objectives, at most three. While we would never recommend every team begin by defining exactly two objectives, we do advise challenging your client to go through the exercise of drafting two objectives to balance internal and external goals.

Some of our clients define two OKRs, an internal OKR and a separate, external OKR. They find it critical to focus on making a positive impact on both external customers and their internal team. *External objectives* are aimed at making an impact outside the team. Nearly all our clients are focused on external objectives. Examples include:

External Objective 1: Win Belgium market.
External Objective 2: Successfully launch add-on product ABC.
External Objective 3: Win more big accounts to accelerate growth.

While customer-facing teams often focus on external objectives, support teams such as HR and finance often have internal objectives. *Internal objectives* are about improving processes that impact our employees and how we can work better as a team. Examples of internal objectives include:[11]

Internal Objective 1: Improve onboarding process for new engineers.
Internal Objective 2: Create a culture of cybersecurity readiness.
Internal Objective 3: Figure out where the money we make comes from.

Questions to ask your client as you help them define how many and what types of objectives to define include:

- If you could only set one objective, would it be internal or external?
- Would it be useful to draft an internal and an external objective?
- Is it acceptable for a team to have only an internal objective even if the top-level OKRs are all external?[12]

Coaching Takeaways

✔ *Less is more.*
  ✔ Limit the number of OKRs when getting started to at most three objectives with four key results per objective.
  ✔ Consider starting with a single OKR per team.
✔ While unusual, certain teams may benefit by defining up to five objectives with up to five key results per objective. These teams define OKRs that reflect nearly all their work to manage expectations about what they will, and will not, deliver in the near term.
✔ Help your client to distinguish between external and internal OKRs.

3. How Will We Score OKRs? How Will We Update Progress?

While scoring key results is essential to success with OKRs, we advise you not to score objectives.[13] In my early years as an OKRs coach, I realized many organizations did not have a clear approach to scoring key results. So, I developed a standard scoring system and named it "Stretch Target Commit."[14] While most of our clients adopt this scoring system, no one approach to scoring key results is ideal for every organization. As a coach you should be familiar with the three most common scoring systems used in the field:

1. **Radical Focus.** Key results are set at a 50% confidence level; key results are achieved or not.
2. **Measure What Matters.** Key results are classified as "commit" or "aspirational." Key results are scored on a 0–1 scale. Commit key results are expected to be fully achieved with a score of 1.0. The target score for aspirational key results is 0.7.
3. **Stretch Target Commit.** Key results are defined by: (1) a stretch with 10% confidence of achievement, (2) a target with 50% confidence, and (3) a commit with 90% confidence.

Regardless of which scoring system your client adopts, be sure they agree to deploy a single system. In several of our early OKRs projects, we provided teams with various options for scoring key results. Several OKRs project leads gave us direct feedback that they would like us to require that all teams adopt a single scoring system when getting started.

Binary Scoring (Oracle)

I first used OKRs in 2011 at a small startup company. We adopted a scoring system based on what worked for Oracle back in the late 1980s. Each key result was either achieved or not. Things were simple. It was binary. If a key result was "Sign 10 new customers by end of quarter" and the quarter ended with nine new customers, the key result was not met. In fact, it was assumed that you'd hit 10 customers midway through the quarter, cross out the 10, raise the bar to 15, and achieve 20 by end of quarter. This approach to key result scoring is known as "set the bar high and overachieve."[15]

It was an unwritten rule that if your team achieved its objectives, your team would be celebrated, and individuals comprising the team would be more likely to be promoted. Your team was successful to the extent that OKRs were achieved.

Oracle's scoring system was not perfect. Consider the previous situation, where the key result was "Sign 10 new customers" but the quarter ended with nine new customers. The binary scoring system could create a sense of failure, as signing nine new customers was interpreted as falling short. Not by much, but still, the feeling was one of losing. Oracle's binary approach based on setting the bar high and overachieving was diametrically opposed to the culture of OKRs at Google, where the worst thing you can do is blow out all your OKRs.

Grading on a 0–1 Scale at End of Cycle (Google)

I learned about how Google *grades*[16] OKRs right about the time the Google Ventures video came out in 2013. The idea was to standardize how all key results are scored across the organization. This normalized scoring model gives everyone a way of knowing how to measure success. A score of zero is bad, a score of 0.3 indicates some progress, a score of 0.7 reflects the target level of achievement, and a score of 1.0 reflects success beyond the target.

The culture at Google emphasizes stretch goals. In fact, scoring all 1s on key results implies gaming the system. I heard a story about a Googler who set lofty goals and then went on to achieve them all. Apparently, everyone assumed he sandbagged. Pranksters brought sandbags into his office as a practical joke.[17] While it might not be perfect, Google's scoring approach standardizes conversations and streamlines communication about the level of achievement for each objective.

Stretch Target Commit with Predefined Scores (Lamorte)

Nearly all organizations score key results at the end of the cycle. Many score key results several intervals throughout the cycle. However, very few define scoring criteria when defining key results. Nearly all our clients find it valuable to establish scoring criteria up front. The conversation about what makes a "0.3" or a "0.7" is more meaningful when we translate these numbers into English. After discussing this with Vincent Drucker – and yes, Vincent is Peter Drucker's son – I developed the guidelines shown in Figure 3.2 that our clients find useful.

	CHARACTERISTICS	QUESTIONS TO ASK
STRETCH	• Equivalent to 1.0 at Google • Most amazing possible outcome • Beyond our control • 10% probability of achievement	**What does *amazing* look like?**
TARGET	• Equivalent to 0.7 at Google • Difficult but attainable • Mostly in our control • 50% probability of achievement	**What do we hope to accomplish?**
COMMIT	• Equivalent to 0.3 at Google • What we expect to achieve • Totally in our control • 90% probability of achievement	**What do we expect to accomplish?**

FIGURE 3.2 Defining a stretch, target, and commit "prescore" for each key result

Here is a story that illustrates the value of aligning on key result scoring up front. The story begins with a VP of engineering creating the following OKR:

> **Objective:** Launch new products to attract new customers.
> **Key Result:** Successfully launch new product ABC as measured by signing up our first 100 paying users by end of Q3.
> 0.3/commit = Prototype tested and approved with launch date in Q4
> 0.7/target = Product launched with first 10 paying users

The key result as written represents the 1.0/stretch scoring level. Aligning on the 0.3/commit and 0.7/target scoring levels before finalizing key results forces a conversation about what is a commitment versus what is a stretch (or aspirational) outcome early in the OKRs cycle. When presented with this scoring model, some of our clients are initially concerned that defining three levels will require too much time. However, in practice, defining these scoring levels takes just minutes.

In this case, the engineering manager let the VP know that the drafted 0.7/target score was not even possible and that the 0.3/commit score would be quite a stretch. The engineering manager had a contact in the legal department who explained that the organization did not have permission to even sell the product until the following quarter. Surprisingly, the VP was not aware of this legal barrier.

The prescoring exercise aligned expectations. It enabled the VP to learn that it would be impossible to get paying users by the end of the quarter. Having these conversations *before* finalizing the key result ensured everyone was on the same page from the start. In this case, to better manage expectations and resources, the engineering team refined the key result. Ironically, the proposed commit level of the key result as drafted by the VP ended up as the stretch level of the finalized key result:

> **Key Result:** Successfully prototype new product ABC as measured by positive feedback from 10 beta users by the end of Q3 with product launch date set in the first half of Q4.
> 0.3/commit = Prototype is launched as measured by feedback from 1 beta tester; product launch date is targeted for Q1.
> 0.7/target = Five beta testers install prototype and provide positive feedback; product launch date set in second half of Q4.

Even though Google uses a 0–1 numerical scoring system, most of our clients do not adopt a numerical scoring scale. Rather than using 0.3, 0.7, and 1.0, they simply use words such as *commit*, *target*, and *stretch* to align on three levels of progress for each key result.

Mid-Cycle Scoring: Historical versus Predictive

Many organizations that approach us for help with OKRs have already started working with OKRs and have implemented a scoring system that focuses on progress to date. As such, they measure historical progress on each key result in the form of "X% complete." While we do not discourage you from looking back and monitoring historical progress on key results, we highly recommend including a predictive element. Let's go back to the "10 new customers" key result to analyze why predictive scoring is so valuable.

Suppose we sign six customers in the first month of the quarter. Great, the key result is 60% complete! However, suppose this same team is not confident that they can sign 10 total customers by quarter end; perhaps the pipeline dried up or a key sales rep just resigned. It would be nice to have a scoring system that communicates this concern.

Predictive scoring serves as an early-warning system to better manage expectations and reduce the surprises many leadership teams would rather avoid. The simplest form of predictive scoring features a single confidence level that a given key result will be achieved or not by the end of the cycle. *Radical Focus* adopts such a system. All key results begin with a confidence score of 5/10 by definition and scores for each key result are updated weekly throughout the cycle. In this case, we could communicate that the confidence score dropped from 50% to just 20% to reflect the unlikelihood of signing 10 customers by quarter end. It is the change that then triggers conversations about progress.[18]

Predictive Scoring That Goes beyond the Numbers

Our analysis of scoring thus far has focused on the actual achievement level of the key result. However, the numerical score of a key result often does not tell the full story. For example, your client may be on track to achieve a key result to onboard five new customers, but achieving the key result requires excessive overtime. The key result champion may provide a high confidence score but feel like saying, "We're on track to achieve the key result, *but . . .*" If there is something that feels bad about the key result, they could flag this by coloring the key result red or selecting a sad-face emoji to escalate and resolve as a team. While some systems use color coding based on numerical scores, other organizations introduce color coding to look beyond the numerical progress of a key result.[19]

One of our clients had a key result to get 100,000 mobile app downloads. They were on track to get 200,000, but the quality of these downloads was horrible. In fact, they were gaming the system by purchasing low-quality downloads to achieve the key result. The key result was not driving the right behavior. Given that the quality was so low, the key result scored a "red 1.0." The opposite case of a "green zero" can also occur.

In the case of a "green zero," there is no progress on the numerical score of the key result, but there is a positive development. Consider the key result, add five new customers this quarter. If your client is on track to add zero customers this quarter, the key result scores a zero.

However, they might have 10 new customers lined up to sign next quarter and feel compelled to color the key result green.

Systems for scoring OKRs are still evolving. We predict that the topic of scoring key results will become more widely discussed as organizations hit a roadblock due to their lack of a clear approach to key result scoring.

Analysis of the Three Most Common Scoring Systems

In the *Radical Focus scoring system,* all key results are set at a 5 in 10 confidence level. It is expected that each team setting OKRs will achieve roughly half of its key results. Key results are updated weekly with a predictive confidence score using a 1–10 rating. Any change in confidence level should trigger conversations. At the end of the period, each key result is either "achieved" or "not achieved." If you achieve 80% of a given key result, it receives a final score of zero. We find teams often achieve "all or nothing." That is, some teams tend to achieve all their key results and others tend to achieve none of them. Teams learn to adjust their level of stretch to better manage expectations as they define future OKRs. Radical Focus scoring often works well for organizations just getting started with OKRs that demand simplicity.

The *Measure What Matters scoring model* requires each key result to be classified as a "commitment" or an "aspiration." At the end of the period, each key result is given a final score, often called a grade, between 0–1. Although this system encourages teams to set both commit and aspirational key results, most teams emphasize commit key results. In our experience, teams adopting this system tend to create commit key results that look like a lengthy to-do list. Aspirational key results, if any are included, are often added as an afterthought. With most key results written as commitments in the form of binary milestones, the scoring process can create confusion. We once saw a final score of 0.4 for the aspirational key result "End Q3 with a permit to build in Portland." What does that even mean?

In the *Stretch Target Commit* approach, all key results are written as stretch outcomes that are typically defined at a confidence level of 1 in 10. The same key result also has a predefined commit and target level. The commit reflects a 9 in 10 confidence level and should be highly controllable with minimal dependence on external factors. The target level reflects a 5 in 10 confidence level, falling somewhere between the commit and stretch.[20] While we find this approach works best in most cases, some organizations benefit by adopting one of the other scoring systems. Figure 3.3 compares the three most common scoring systems.

	Radical Focus (Wodtke)	Measure What Matters (Doerr)	Stretch Target Commit (Lamorte)
What it is	KRs are set at a 5 in 10 confidence level.	KRs are classified as commit or aspirational.	KRs include stretch, commit, and target.
When to use	When your client demands **simplicity**.	When OKRs are intended primarily to drive **accountability**.	When your client wants to create a **stretch culture** that focuses on *outcomes, not output.*
Strength	**Simple:** One standard scoring level for all KRs throughout the entire organization.	**Accountability:** There is a clear expectation that commit KRs will be 100% achieved.	**Stretch & Alignment:** Forces stretch thinking for each KR with a commit and target level to **manage expectations.**
Limitation	**Ambiguous mid-cycle scoring:** What if we are 100% sure we will achieve 80% of a given key result. Is this 0/10 or 8/10?	**Too many OKRs:** KRs are often written as a to-do list rather than a focused set of aspirational KRs.	**Too ambitious:** Writing stretch outcomes may not work for teams looking to use OKRs to focus on commitments.
Focuses on evaluation or communication & learning	**Communication & Learning:** Changes in confidence trigger conversations.	**Evaluation:** KRs get final grades with a 0-1 score. Grades may be used to evaluate performance.	**Communication & Learning:** Scoring at each step of the cycle communicates expectations.

FIGURE 3.3 Comparing the three most common systems for scoring key results

Coaching Takeaways

✔ It is not the purpose of scoring key results to evaluate employee performance. It is to (1) communicate targets, (2) manage expectations, and (3) enable learning.
✔ Select a single system for scoring key results when getting started.
✔ Consider adding a "quality" dimension using colors or happy/sad emojis to promote check-in conversations that go beyond the numbers.
✔ We recommend the Stretch Target Commit system to align on achievement levels and manage expectations *before* publishing key results.

4. How Long Is an OKRs Cycle?

The first OKRs cycle varies from a rapid, one-month pilot cycle on up to a full year. We recommend avoiding a one-month cycle as it is difficult to write OKRs for such a short period. Encourage your client to adopt a common cycle time when getting started. Beginning with a single cycle time ensures each team completes a cycle together and shares learnings along the way. Most teams define OKRs on a quarterly basis. However, as noted in the introduction, some organizations prefer a four-month cycle to avoid holiday delays and the quarterly crunch.

After using OKRs for a year or so, many organizations do not require a single cycle time for all teams.[21] While most teams stick to the default timing, other teams may adjust their cycle time after completing a cycle or two. This is especially common for teams like research and development that require more time to make measurable progress. In addition, the default cycle duration may vary depending on the level within the organization. Higher-level OKRs tend to be more strategic and therefore are defined for a longer period. OKRs at lower levels in the organization tend to be more operational and are often set for shorter durations.

Top-level objectives often do not change throughout the course of a year. In fact, keeping top-level objectives consistent quarter over quarter can be a good thing. This consistency provides workers at lower levels in the organization more time to understand top-level objectives and use them as context for creating their team's OKRs.

Team-level OKRs tend to be defined quarterly or on four-month cycles, but this is not required. Some organizations define several layers of team-level OKRs with various cycle times. One of our larger clients in the banking sector had three levels for team OKRs. They referred to each of the three levels as "tiers." Tier 1 teams set annual objectives with annual key results that were reviewed quarterly. Tier 2 teams set annual objectives with key results defined for a six-month period with quarterly check-ins. Tier 3 teams set quarterly objectives with quarterly key results and conducted their check-ins midway through the quarter.[22]

> **Coaching Takeaways**
>
> ✔ Align on a single cycle time for the first OKRs cycle.
> ✔ While organizations often define a three-month cycle time, explore a four-month cycle with clients seeking to avoid holiday delays and the quarterly crunch.
> ✔ Large organizations with several levels of OKRs tend to define shorter cycle times at lower levels.

5. What Are the Three Types of Key Results? Are Milestones Appropriate?

There are three types of key results: metric, baseline, and milestone. Metric key results are the most common. They look like "move metric A from X to Y." Baseline key results are used when X is not being measured and your client seeks a metric to reflect progress on a given objective. Your client should only put in the effort to establish a baseline if they expect to use that baseline as the starting point for a metric key result in a future OKRs cycle.[23] Most leadership teams define a solid set of metric key results for top-level objectives. However, many teams struggle to define metric key results.

Dozens of teams send us their OKRs for feedback each year. Their key results often look more like a list of tasks that reflect work output rather than measurable outcomes. Unlike metric key results, milestone key results tend not to include numbers. Milestones are binary – they are either achieved or not. Given that milestones are notorious for reflecting work output rather than outcomes, should milestone key results even be allowed?

Some OKRs coaches advise avoiding milestone key results entirely. On page seven of his OKRs book, John Doerr credits Marissa Mayer with her observation, "It's not a key result unless it has a number." However, in this same book, Doerr provides examples of milestone key results such as "Develop a demo."[24] Marissa might not be happy with this key result! As an OKRs coach, you work with your client to transform draft key results that often look like a to-do list into refined key results that reflect measurable outcomes. Here is a hypothetical OKRs coaching conversation to make this concrete:

Client: My key result is to develop a demo.

Coach: What is the intended outcome of developing this demo? How will we know the demo is a success?

Client: Well, the demo is a success if we can get positive customer feedback, but all I can commit to is developing the demo this quarter. It will be quite a stretch to get feedback.

Coach: OK, what will be demo'd and how will we know it is developed?

Client: We're developing a demo for product X and our sales team decides if it's developed and ready to be used. Ultimately, it is our customers that will decide if it's a valuable product.

Coach: Are you committing to presenting the demo to the sales team or to customers?

Client: I can't commit to showing it to customers. That is the decision of the sales team. I can commit to presenting the demo to our sales team.

A bit more OKRs coaching might lead to the following refined key result that (1) focuses on outcome, (2) distinguishes between a commitment and a stretch outcome, and (3) specifies what is being "demo'd" and who decides it is "developed."

> **Key Result:** Three customers sign an agreement to purchase product X after viewing the new product X demo.
> **Commit** = Present product X demo to our sales team for feedback in our test environment.
> **Target** = Present product X demo to five prospects with feedback on likelihood to purchase.

In this hypothetical coaching conversation, the draft key result, "Develop a demo," becomes the commit level of progress. However, the stretch key result now reflects customer interest in the product. It is the number of customers interested in the product that reflects the needle the client is ultimately trying to move. Marissa would likely approve now that the key result has a number.

As an OKRs coach, you help your client translate milestone key results like "produce a demo of product X" into aspirational outcomes like "three customers sign an agreement for product X" that move a metric rather than simply represent completion of a task. Therefore, we might conclude that all key results should be metrics. However, while we recommend defining mostly metric key results, our clients often choose to define milestone key results as well.

Rather than declaring all milestone key results are bad, we invite you to consider the possibility that milestone key results can be used to reflect *outcomes, not output*. Consider the following two milestone key results one of our clients drafted: (1) Present requirements to obtain a permit to build houses in Portland to leadership team; and (2) Obtain a permit to begin new construction in Portland. The first milestone is a task that reflects work output. One person should be able to research required documentation for a permit and schedule a meeting with leadership. However, the second milestone is not a task; it is a potential key result that reflects a binary outcome. Ask questions to guide your client to move from task-like milestones that reflect work output to key results that reflect outcomes.

Coaching Takeaways

✔ **Metrics.** Help your client define mostly metric key results (i.e., move metric A from X to Y).

✔ **Baselines.** If your client is not already measuring the right metric to capture progress on an objective, consider defining a baseline key result. In other words, "Find X" so your client can define a metric key result to improve from X to Y in the future.

✔ **Milestones.** Not all milestone key results are bad! Ask questions to help move your client further down the value chain to translate tasks and work output into outcomes.

✔ **Use scoring to convert output milestones to outcome milestones or metrics.** As inspiration, use the hypothetical coaching conversation that translated the output milestone, "Develop a demo," into the metric key result, "Three customers sign an agreement to purchase product X after viewing the new product X demo."

6. Where Will We Draft, Publish, and Track OKRs?

When I got started as an OKRs coach, my clients and I included the word "DRAFT" in all capital letters at the top of each team's OKRs drafting template. As each team refined their OKRs, they did so in their own drafting template in Microsoft Word. Each team published their OKRs in a single spreadsheet only when they were final. Today, our clients still prefer to draft OKRs in one environment and publish their final OKRs in a single location, most often a spreadsheet. Many of our clients still use Microsoft Word (or Google Docs) for drafting and Microsoft Excel (or Google Sheets) for publishing.

As the initial wave of OKRs software applications gained traction in 2015, to our knowledge none of them supported a "draft mode." In other words, once you typed your OKRs into the system, there they were. The CEO of one OKRs software solution suggested that drafting OKRs into the software right from the start would keep things lightweight and be great for collaboration. This CEO felt that adding a "draft mode" would just add more work and make the process too complex. In practice, we find that many of our clients are not comfortable entering their OKRs into a transparent software system until their OKRs are reviewed and approved. Even worse, if draft OKRs are entered into the software, there is no way to know which OKRs are final and which are still in draft mode. Keeping draft OKRs separate from the published set of OKRs resonates with all our clients.[25]

Be flexible when drafting OKRs. We advise providing your client with an OKRs drafting template.[26] Most of our clients encourage their teams to use whatever environment feels most comfortable when drafting OKRs. However, all our clients require OKRs be published in the same format in a single location. Documenting all OKRs in one location helps drive visibility, accountability, and alignment. We refer to this single location as the "OKRs tracker."[27]

Advise your client to create their own OKRs tracker prior to exploring dedicated OKRs software. You can help your client create and even populate their OKRs tracker in an hour or two. About once a month, an organization approaches us right after purchasing a dedicated OKRs application before even attempting to define their OKRs. Somehow, these organizations purchased software to help automate a process that they did not yet have in place. We advise completing at least one OKRs cycle with several pilot teams prior to shopping for OKRs software. Once your OKRs process is established, it often makes sense to explore software to automate and scale that process.

Coaching Takeaways

✔ Provide your client with an OKRs drafting template.

✔ Be flexible when drafting OKRs; use whatever is easiest for your client (e.g., Microsoft Word, Google Docs, or even a whiteboard).

✔ Publish all OKRs in one place, the OKRs tracker.

✔ Establish an OKRs process for at least one cycle before shopping for software to automate and scale that process.

7. How Will OKRs Relate to Performance Reviews?

Be sure to involve your client's HR leadership and executive sponsor to align on how best to relate OKRs to performance reviews. While there is no one right answer to this question, let's agree on two wrong answers.

The first wrong answer is that OKRs are the official system for performance reviews and compensation. As OKRs are designed to reflect stretch thinking, it should be obvious that an OKRs program is doomed from the start if OKRs are the basis for determining incentive compensation and evaluation of staff.

To ensure that OKRs are not interpreted as the performance management system itself, advise your clients not to define OKRs at the individual level when getting started. Defining OKRs only at the company or team levels makes it clear that OKRs are distinct from individual performance evaluation. We advise caution when using HR software that tracks both performance review data and OKRs. Employees that access such integrated HR tools often report that managing OKRs and performance reviews in a single tool makes OKRs and performance reviews feel as if they are a single system. Our clients also struggle when introducing OKRs and a new performance review process concurrently, as this conflates the two systems.

The second wrong answer is that OKRs have absolutely nothing to do with performance reviews and compensation. An executive at a leading tech company was once asked what he wished he had done differently after launching a successful OKRs program. He answered, "I wish I didn't say that OKRs are decoupled from performance management. That's just what I thought I was supposed to say based on watching the Google Video on OKRs." He went on to explain that OKRs and performance management should be distinct but related. So, the question becomes what does "distinct but related" mean? We are right back to our original question: How should OKRs be related with performance?

Begin by interviewing your client to learn about their existing performance management system if such a system is in place. Next, consider the following two principles that resonate with all organizations that take time to define how OKRs relate to performance reviews and incentive compensation:

1. OKRs *should* be included in performance review discussions via structured questions to position managers as coaches.
2. Scores on key results *should not* be used to calculate bonuses.

Principle 1: OKRs Should Be Included in Performance Review Discussions via Structured Questions to Position Managers as Coaches

Given that team-level OKRs reflect a focus for improvement, it is only natural that individual performance reviews incorporate a structured discussion of their team's OKRs. We advise our clients to consider incorporating OKRs-related questions into their performance review process. These questions are informed by why they have chosen to implement OKRs. In addition, managers may bring these questions into 1:1s with their direct reports.[28] Here are sample questions our clients have adopted to address impact, focus, communication, and learning:

Impact. Which key result/s do you feel you impacted?
Focus. How did you use OKRs to focus on high-priority work?
Communication. How did you leverage OKRs to better communicate?
Learning. Which key result did you learn from? How will you apply this learning going forward?

While some organizations include OKRs questions in their formal performance reviews, others distinguish between a performance review 1:1 and an OKRs review 1:1. One of our clients already had a quarterly performance review process in place. They happened to define a four-month OKRs cycle time. This client stumbled into two unexpected benefits resulting from these distinct time frames: (1) it was easier to decouple OKRs from the performance review process; and (2) an increase in the number of structured 1:1 conversations from four to seven each year.

Managers can certainly have more than seven such 1:1s over the course of the year, but these seven touch points are required and documented with HR. While there may be some overlap between OKRs and performance management, there is an agreement to address OKRs and performance management in separate meetings. This approach may resonate with your client if they are looking to create more engagement between managers and their direct reports.

Principle 2: Scores on Key Results Should Not Be Used to Calculate Incentive Compensation

Incentive compensation should be calculated independently of OKRs. Some key results may not connect to incentive compensation at all. Other key results may correlate with bonuses. For example, the value of a metric key result based on revenue is often used as part of a bonus calculation. That's fine. It is the value of the metric key result that determines compensation, not the score. The distinction is subtle, but important. OKRs should enable us to think big as we align on stretch goals. Linking key result scores to compensation creates incentives to set low targets and may reinforce silo thinking. Two examples are:

Example 1: Key result value (not score) tied to bonus

Sales key result: Increase new sales from $1,000,000 to $2,000,000 this quarter (pre-scoring: commit = $800,000; target = $1,200,000)

In this case, the sales team is paid a bonus based on revenue from new sales, so the actual *value* of this metric is directly correlated to the bonus. However, bonuses are not determined based on whether a *score* of commit, target, or stretch is achieved. The bonus is calculated based on the value of the actual metric itself.

Example 2: Key result not tied to bonus

Human resources key result: Increase the number of phone screens for VP candidates from 40 last month to 80 this month (prescoring: commit = 40; target = 60)

In this case, there were no bonuses calculated based on the number of candidates screened over the phone. This is still an important metric to the organization, but neither the scores on the key result nor the value of this metric determine bonus payout.

Coaching Takeaways

DO. . .

- ✔ **Assess existing approach.** Have a conversation with your client's HR lead to learn about the existing performance review system if such a system is in place.
- ✔ **Connect OKRs with performance management.** In addition to OKRs project leads, include the HR lead and executive sponsor to align on how your client will connect OKRs with performance management.
- ✔ **Bring OKRs into performance reviews.** If your client has a performance system in place, advise your client to consider incorporating structured OKRs questions into their performance review process.

DO NOT. . .

- ✔ **Use key result scores to calculate bonus.** Using key result scores as the basis for calculating incentive compensation discourages stretch thinking.
- ✔ **Roll out both systems together.** Rolling out OKRs and a new performance management system at the same time creates confusion and even anxiety.
- ✔ **Begin with individual-level OKRs.** Starting with individual-level OKRs blurs the distinction between OKRs and performance evaluation.

8. How Are OKRs Different from KPIs?

If your client is already using key performance indicators to evaluate performance or make calculations for incentive compensation, they must distinguish between OKRs and KPIs. However, many of our clients report KPIs, even though they do not have a formal performance review process in place. Such organizations tend to worry about how and if they can integrate OKRs with KPIs. They often worry that the two systems are either redundant or are somehow in conflict. Here is a high-level overview followed by a detailed comparison of KPIs and OKRs.

High-Level Overview: OKRs versus KPIs

Based on our experience with hundreds of organizations that use KPIs, we can tell you one thing about KPIs for certain: the term "KPI" does not have a standard definition. Some companies use *KPI* interchangeably with *metric*. That is, every metric that is reported is also referred to as a KPI. While some companies have just one KPI, others have thousands.[29] Some organizations use KPIs as the basis for calculating incentive compensation for all staff while other organizations define KPIs to evaluate performance of the overall company and do not even offer incentive compensation.

Unlike KPIs, key results do have a standard definition. Key results answer the question, "How will we know we've made measurable progress on a specific objective by a certain date?"

Organizations with an established KPI system in place often ask if they should replace KPIs with OKRs. The fact that they are asking this question reflects a deep misunderstanding. Choosing between OKRs and KPIs is a false choice. OKRs and KPIs work together in tandem. A given KPI is a key result if it is the focus for near-term improvement. A KPI is classified as a health metric if it is important to monitor but is not the focus for near-term improvement. Metric key results are typically based on underlying KPIs.

To illustrate how OKRs and KPIs work together, consider a company with the objective: "Achieve financial targets" and the following three key results:

1. Double **company revenue** from $5M in Q1 to $10M in Q2.
2. Increase **gross profit margin** from 20% in Q1 to 25% in Q2.
3. Increase **recurring revenue** from existing install base from $400k in Q1 to $600k in Q2.

Each of these metric key results has the **KPI in bold** built in. In fact, metric key results equate to moving a given KPI from X to Y within a set time frame.

At the team level, milestone key results are more prevalent. Milestone key results do not translate directly to KPIs. Differentiating between metric and milestone key results helps clarify how OKRs and KPIs work together. Suppose a marketing department has the following OKR:

Objective: Make growth more sustainable.
Key Results:

1. Launch marketing automation system as measured by sending our first set of nurture emails by the end of Q1.
2. Reduce **marketing cost per lead** from $100 in Q4 to $95 by end of Q1.

Notice that **marketing cost per lead**, in bold, is a KPI at the marketing team level. However, "sending our first set of nurture emails" is unlikely to be classified as a KPI; this statement is classified as a milestone key result. Although a milestone key result is not defined as movement of a numerical KPI from X to Y, milestone key results should be designed to impact a KPI in the future. For example, achieving the milestone of launching a marketing automation system may not impact marketing cost per lead in the current period. However, it is expected to have an impact on a KPI in the future, as illustrated in Figure 3.4.

Milestone   **Metric**

FIGURE 3.4   A milestone key result designed to impact a KPI in the future

Detailed Analysis of KPIs versus OKRs

The original question of how OKRs differs from KPIs is better framed as: "How do *key results* differ from key performance indicators?" Objectives are qualitative statements, and as such, should not be confused with quantitative KPIs. To distinguish between KPIs and key results, some of our clients like to include a chart like the one shown in Figure 3.5 in their OKRs training materials.

Distinguishing Factor	Key Result	KPI
Defined in context of an objective?	Always, by definition	Sometimes
Achievement tied to compensation?	Sometimes	Often
Visible to all employees?	Almost always	Sometimes
Focused on maintenance work and health metrics?	Rarely	Often
Intended to increase alignment across teams?	Often	Rarely
Informs near-term focus and prioritization?	Often	Sometimes
Controllable by a single team?	Somewhat	Mostly
Originates from team members?	Mostly	Rarely

FIGURE 3.5   Distinguishing between key results and KPIs

Defined in Context of an Objective?

The most obvious difference between key results and KPIs is the fact that key results are defined in the context of an objective. The objectives that contain key results should include a brief analysis of why the objective is so important now. While KPIs are sometimes defined in context of higher-level goals, they often lack context and appear as a list of metrics to quantify the performance of some part of the organization.

Achievement Tied to Compensation?

While KPIs are often designed specifically to determine incentive compensation structures, OKRs are not. OKRs should be decoupled from compensation. While scores on OKRs should not be used as the basis for determining incentive compensation, OKRs are often incorporated, qualitatively, as part of the performance review process. The most critical reason for separating OKRs from incentive compensation goes back to Andy Grove's original intent that OKRs should be stretch goals.

Visible to All Employees?

Management by Objectives (MBOs), Andy Grove's inspiration for creating the OKRs model, is often used as a system for determining incentive compensation. Thus, MBOs are often kept secret between manager and employee. Similarly, KPIs are often tied to compensation and may therefore be kept private between manager and employee.

Andy Grove wanted to take the MBO model to the next level. Grove insisted that OKRs be made visible across the entire organization. The fact that everyone can see a set of well-defined goals in a standard format sets the stage for alignment. With OKRs, the question is not whether to make them visible. The question is to what extent.[30]

Most coaches advise their clients to make OKRs visible across the entire organization. However, some of our clients begin their OKRs programs by giving access to OKRs only to certain groups of employees, for example, director and above.[31] Given that nearly all organizations decide to make OKRs visible to all staff by default, we do not consider this a universal deployment parameter. Nonetheless, as some organizations choose to specify restrictions, we've added visibility to the list of "other deployment parameters" at the end of this chapter.

Focused on Maintenance Work and Health Metrics?

Many organizations classify every metric they measure as a KPI. However, the fact that you are measuring something does not make it a key result. If we think of KPIs as the set of metrics a company measures, then a KPI is either a key result or a health metric.

A given KPI is classified as a key result if the company decides to focus on improving the value of the KPI in the near term. If a KPI is not the focus for near-term improvement, it is classified as a health metric. Health metrics are already within an acceptable range. For example, while website uptime may be a KPI, if the website is currently at 99.99% uptime, it is unlikely to be a key result that is a focus for near-term improvement. Does it really make sense to define a key result to drive a team to "improve website uptime from 99.99% to 99.999%"?

Intended to Increase Alignment across Teams?

KPIs are often created to measure a given team's performance. Team members care a lot about their own team's KPIs. However, they are often disinterested in the extent to which other teams achieve their KPIs. In fact, a team member might even get a feeling of superiority when their team achieves its KPIs and other teams do not. Conversely, the OKRs framework seeks to get employees working together to make measurable progress. OKRs are often defined and shared across functional teams. As noted in the first deployment parameter, defining OKRs may even lead to the formation of cross-functional squads.

Informs Near-Term Focus and Prioritization?

KPIs do not require a specific time frame. They are simply metrics such as "revenue," "room nights booked," and "net promoter score." KPIs may or may not have target values within a set time frame. As KPIs include health metrics, lists of KPIs can become massive. KPIs are often intended to be reported in dashboards rather than to communicate the near-term priorities.

Conversely, key results articulate how an organization will measure progress of an objective within a set time frame. While KPIs tend to stick around year after year, most key results are modified or removed as part of the reflect and reset step in the OKRs cycle.

Controllable by a Single Team?

Given KPIs are often used to evaluate a team's performance, it is only natural that KPIs tend to be totally controllable by a single team. However, key results are often written as amazing outcomes. Amazing outcomes tend to depend on external factors that may not be totally controllable by a single team. And that's fine. Both *Measure What Matters* and the Stretch Target Commit scoring systems define "commit" key results that should be mostly controllable by the team. Nonetheless, all scoring systems, including *Radical Focus*, advocate setting key results that stretch teams out of their comfort zone rather than what they feel is completely within their control.

Originates from Team Members?

As KPIs are often used to measure performance and even determine bonuses, they tend to come from the top. While most objectives come from the top, most key results originate from team members rather than the boss. To clarify, some key results will (and should) come from top-level leadership. However, the process of creating key results involves a dialog between team members and leadership. This leads us nicely into our last two universal parameters where we explore how to align OKRs and ensure that most key results originate bottom-up.

Coaching Takeaways

✔ OKRs and KPIs work together; they are not conflicting systems.
✔ Unlike key results, KPIs do not have a standard definition.
✔ A KPI is considered a key result when it is the focus for near-term improvement.
✔ A KPI that is not the focus for near-term improvement is a health metric.
✔ Use Figure 3.5 as inspiration to create training materials that help your clients distinguish between KPIs and key results.

---

9. How Will We Ensure OKRs Are Aligned?

Before exploring how to help your client ensure that their OKRs are aligned, let's look at the wrong approach, the direct cascade. This approach begins with OKRs at the highest level, which is a good thing. However, in a direct cascade, lower-level OKRs are required to be subsets of higher-level OKRs. John Doerr provided the OKRs community with a great example of a direct cascade with his hypothetical football team example. This example illustrates how higher-level key results become the objectives for teams at lower levels.[32]

We have seen several OKRs software vendors demonstrate how OKRs cascade to illustrate the simplicity of aligning OKRs at every level in an organization. We have even seen presentations of the direct cascade that refer to higher-level key results as "parents of lower-level child objectives." While it is appealing in theory, the practice of cascading OKRs is rarely, if ever, a viable approach for aligning OKRs.

The direct cascade approach violates two foundational elements of OKRs. First, it implies that a higher-level key result becomes the objective for a lower-level department or team as shown in Figure 3.6. This violates the fundamental distinction between an objective and a key result. An objective is broad and qualitative; a key result is measurable and quantitative. Objectives are measured by the achievement of their underlying key results; however, key results should not be measured by achievement of an underlying objective.

The direct cascade approach also violates a second foundational element, as it inherently does not engage lower-level teams. Lower-level teams begin their drafting sessions by copying and pasting OKRs from higher levels. They are forced to choose from a list of predefined options rather than creating and aligning on their team's objective through critical thinking.

A direct cascade might work for an organization seeking to use OKRs to reinforce a hierarchical culture. The direct cascade provides a visual chart that illustrates how OKRs are connected from

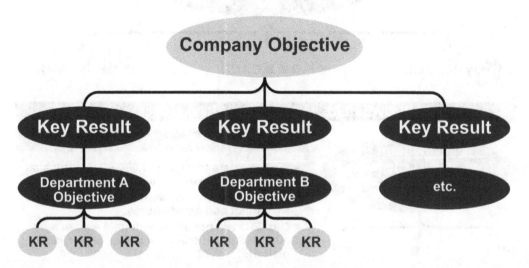

FIGURE 3.6 The direct cascade approach in which parent key results have objectives as their children

the top down. In theory, this approach holds lower-level workers accountable for impacting higher-level goals and enables all teams to see how they contribute to top-level goals. However, every organization that we have seen attempt to implement the direct cascade approach has failed. Even worse, we often find cascading OKRs reduces cross-functional alignment. If each top-level key result is designed to be owned by a single team, then each team simply focuses on their assignments and returns to their silos. So, if the direct cascade doesn't work, what does?

We recommend that each team documents how their objectives are aligned to top-level strategy (and/or horizontally aligned with other teams) as part of their analysis of why their team's objectives are important now. Team leads and executives have conversations to confirm objectives are aligned. Figure 3.7 illustrates how a data platform team confirmed that their team's OKR was aligned even though it did not connect to a higher-level OKR. In this case, it was the conversation, not a set of arrows, that confirmed alignment. We chose this example because alignment is not even possible with a direct cascade.

The data platform team did not create their objective by copying and pasting a higher-level key result. Instead, they leveraged the OKRs critical thinking framework and agreed as a

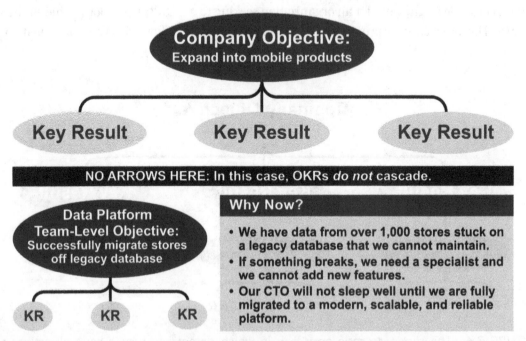

FIGURE 3.7   Using "Why now?" to align OKRs instead of a direct cascade

team that migrating stores off a legacy database was the most important area to focus on making measurable progress in the near term. Next, the data platform team lead discussed the proposed objective with the CEO and presented why it was such an important objective right now. Alignment happened the moment the CEO agreed with the data platform lead. Alignment did not require a set of arrows showing how the OKR cascaded from a higher-level OKR. The data platform team's objective was still valid even though it did not relate to the company's objective to expand into mobile products.

This section concludes with the three-step process used at Huawei to ensure OKRs are aligned. Huawei emphasizes OKRs discussions to align on OKRs rather than a direct cascade. We find Huawei's approach insightful, as OKRs are set for teams and individuals.

While we generally do not advise setting OKRs at the individual level, Huawei has found a way to make this work. Huawei embraces the fact that higher-level OKRs do not attempt to capture all work at lower levels. They expand the definition of OKRs at the individual level to capture work that does not connect to higher-level OKRs. Individual contributors prioritize their work and are validated even if they do not contribute to higher-level OKRs.

CONTRIBUTION: **ALIGNING OKRs AT HUAWEI**

Kuang Yang, Huawei OKRs project lead and OKRs author

At Huawei, we have a three-step process to ensure OKRs are aligned.

First, the leader gathers all team members into a meeting room to discuss team OKRs. In this meeting, the leader summarizes results from the last period and provides some direction for the next period. Shortly thereafter, team members discuss and refine objectives and key results inspired by the leader's summary and higher-level OKRs.

Second, once team-level OKRs are fixed, team members each set individual OKRs and align them to their team's OKRs. In most cases, individual OKRs align to the team's OKRs. However, strict alignment is not required. If there is not a clear alignment to a higher-level OKR, the individual team member and leader have a conversation to align on the given individual's OKRs. In such cases, the individual's OKRs are often focused on maintaining health metrics or performing compliance activities that may not be reflected in team-level OKRs.

Third, once the OKRs are set, we upload all OKRs to our OKRs tracker platform. With all OKRs in a single location, anyone can read and comment on anyone else's OKRs, including the leader's. If someone doesn't agree with your OKRs, they can add comments as well.

Coaching Takeaways

DO. . .

✔ Use higher-level OKRs as context for creating lower-level OKRs.

✔ Encourage your client to specify how lower-level objectives connect to top-level goals as part of the "Why now?" analysis of each objective.

✔ Discuss lower-level OKRs with leadership to confirm alignment.

DO NOT. . .

✔ Use the direct cascade approach to define OKRs.

✔ Turn a key result into a lower-level team's objective.

✔ Copy and paste higher-level OKRs to define lower-level OKRs.

10. How Do We Ensure Team Members Define Most Key Results "Bottom-Up"?

Everyone we know in the OKRs community agrees that most key results should include input from team members rather than be mandated by the boss. When OKRs are working well, team members often feel like their ideas help shape goals. Taking a more bottom-up approach is essential to creating engagement in the OKRs development process as well as driving alignment. Some organizations take an extreme top-down or bottom-up approach.

We met one CEO who wrote down OKRs for each team across the entire company, presented these OKRs, and then asked, "Any questions?" In this extreme top-down approach to OKRs, the CEO simply developed OKRs in isolation and issued a command. Team members felt excluded from the OKRs drafting process.

On the other extreme, we encountered a CEO who took a completely bottom-up approach. We facilitated a workshop with all 150 employees at this company and took several hours drafting company-level OKRs. While this approach engaged everyone, we do not generally recommend this approach, as it is not efficient to develop top-level OKRs with such a massive group. So, how can your client find their ideal balance between these two extremes? Here is what we find works best in practice.

Team leads often create objectives and present them to their team as context at the start of an OKRs drafting workshop. The team lead often solicits input on the objective from higher-level executives prior to the drafting workshop to confirm alignment. Then, with the essence of the objective in place, team members draft most of the key results. Some leaders choose to remain in the room but let the team members drive the process. Other leaders choose to introduce objectives, align on why each objective is important, then leave the room to allow team members to think freely about key results. In this approach, the team leader returns to the room a couple hours later, or the next day, to review and refine OKRs with team members.

Some organizations choose a purely top-down approach to defining OKRs just for their first cycle. They intentionally emphasize the top-down approach, so that leadership gets comfortable with how OKRs work before scaling the program. They then engage team members in the second cycle. This approach works because the first cycle introduces team members to OKRs in the context of their actual OKRs. Not surprisingly, these team members provide feedback that their first cycle failed because it was too top-down. However, these team members are then quite engaged and happy to contribute to helping shape their team's OKRs for the next cycle. By the end of the second or third cycle, these teams use OKRs as a framework for aligning on the areas to focus on making measurable improvement.

Coaching Takeaways

- ✔ Team leads define most objectives.
- ✔ Team members provide input to help define most key results.
- ✔ When teams draft OKRs, team leads set the stage by introducing each objective, as well as why each objective is so important right now.
- ✔ Consider starting completely top-down to ensure leadership gets comfortable with OKRs with the plan of introducing a more bottom-up approach in the second cycle.

Other Deployment Parameters

We just analyzed 10 universal deployment parameters in detail. We advise you to take time to address all 10 in every engagement as part of Phase 1. While these universal parameters may be sufficient for some organizations, take a step back before moving on to Phase 2. Go over the deployment plan with your OKRs project lead and executive sponsor. Ask your client if they are ready to announce their deployment plan.[33] Remind your client that organizations often define additional parameters to reflect their unique culture and approach to OKRs. It might help to provide a few examples to your client to get them thinking. Some other parameters are:

How can we ensure our key results balance quantity with quality?

How do we balance leading and lagging indicators?

At what level in the organization will OKRs be made visible?

How will we deal with dependencies on India?

Shall we specify where we are choosing to not allocate resources?[34]

 NOTES

1. The football example is detailed later in this chapter. It is misleading because OKRs do not directly cascade.
2. One of our clients was concerned with resource allocation between India and the US, so they decided to add a region parameter. All their key results were tagged as "India" or "USA." Clearly this is not a universal parameter.
3. Ideally, each individual employee should be able to articulate why leadership wants to implement OKRs and how they can benefit from OKRs as an individual. To this end, we are seeing more and more organizations add questions about how (and to what extent) the use of OKRs is beneficial as part of their employee engagement surveys.
4. Marty Cagan, *Inspired* (John Wiley and Sons, 2017), p. 144.
5. We have seen several sets of individual-level OKRs used at Google. One memorable key result reflected a personal goal to "buy a 3-bedroom house in Mountain View." Should OKRs be a place to capture personal goals for all staff? We think not.
6. For more on the pros and cons (mostly cons) of setting individual OKRs, see Paul Niven and Ben Lamorte, *Objectives and Key Results: Driving Focus Alignment, and Engagement with OKRs* (John Wiley and Sons, 2016), pp. 101–102.
7. Refer to the ninth deployment parameter in this chapter to see how individuals at Huawei align their OKRs to higher-level OKRs and health metrics.

8. One of our clients required every team to define exactly three objectives with exactly three key results per objective. The OKRs project leads quickly implemented our advice to make this less restrictive. They modified their guidance to "at most three objectives with a total of at most nine key results per team."

9. Some of our clients ask each team to estimate the percentage of their effort that will be allocated to OKRs versus other work.

10. Christina Wodtke is the most prominent OKRs expert recommending a single OKR.

11. To see "Why now?" for these three internal objectives, refer to step 3 of the seven steps for creating OKRs in Chapter 5. To see "Why now?" for the three external objectives, refer to the sample email in Chapter 4.

12. We say this is possible! Alignment is based on a conversation rather than a mathematical or logical relationship. Refer to Figure 3.7 for an example.

13. We often hear from organizations that scoring objectives creates more problems than it solves. At best, the process is a waste of time. Some organizations build charts based on objective scores to stack rank team performance. These ranking charts defeat the purpose of OKRs, penalizing teams for aiming high and forcing teams to defend low scores rather than emphasizing learning. If you or anyone you know can report a positive impact from scoring objectives, please email me via Ben@OKRs.com.

14. My scoring system was originally called "aspirational with prescoring." We changed the name to "stretch target commit" in 2021 based on client feedback. For more on scoring, see this YouTube interview: https://youtu.be/xMRlI6cJwQg.

15. Source: Private discussions with Jeff Walker, who referred to "set the bar high and overachieve" as the cultural approach to OKRs while he served as CFO of Oracle in the late 1980s.

16. Note Google's use of the word *grade*. This word is often used interchangeably with *score*. We use "score" because "grade" emphasizes evaluation rather than learning. We believe OKRs should focus on learning more than evaluation.

17. This story is taken from John Doerr's presentation at the 2015 Goal Summit in San Francisco. Whether the story is true or not does not matter; it's the spirit of the story that is relevant.

18. Here's what Christina Wodtke has to say on this topic: "If you set a confidence of five out of ten, has that moved up or down? Have a discussion about why." Christina Wodtke, *Radical Focus: Achieving Your Most Important Goals with Objectives and Key Results* (Boxes and Arrows, 2017).

19. The *Measure What Matters* approach often equates a key result's numerical score to a color of red, yellow, or green. The color does not capture data about how the key result champion is feeling about the key result beyond the numbers. I was lucky enough to work with Joel Trammel and the team at Khorus who were early promoters of a two-dimensional scoring system that he referred to as "likelihood and quality."

20. Instead of writing each key result as a stretch outcome, some of our clients prefer to write each key result as a target level. They then specify the commit and stretch levels of progress in parentheses. Take whichever approach works best for your client, just be sure to be consistent.

21. Our clients find it best to stick to a single cycle time for the first cycle to optimize learning. You may want to even require everyone to stay on the same cycle time for a second cycle. However, if a given team wants to deviate from the default cycle time, we recommend having that conversation instead of simply requiring all teams stick to a single cycle time.

22. Continuing with this logic, individual-level OKRs, if they are part of an organization's OKRs program, tend to be defined for extremely short time frames. In fact, Mulyadi Oey, an OKRs Coach Network founding member based in Indonesia, finds that individuals often benefit by defining super-short OKRs cycles of a week or two.

23. For more on baseline key results, refer to the first coaching excerpt in Chapter 1 and the NPS story in the Epilogue.

24. In reviewing John Doerr's book, Felipe Castro, an OKRs expert and good friend of mine, notes: "Out of the 60 Key Results listed, 32 (53%) lack numbers. They include things such as "Create a retirement plan for all legacy technology," and "Focus on hiring player managers/leaders." Even John Doerr's own OKRs from his days at Intel lack numbers (e.g., "Develop a Demo").

25. Good news: We confirmed in 2020 that at least one OKRs software tool now offers draft mode.

26. Refer to the Epilogue for a sample OKRs drafting handout.

27. Refer to Chapter 5 for more on the OKRs tracker and how to use it with your client throughout the OKRs cycle.

28. We advise you review page 269 of *Measure What Matters* by John Doerr for additional questions that managers can ask their direct reports in Resource 3, All Talk: Performance Conversations.

29. One of our clients had the single KPI, "room nights booked." Everyone in the company knew the goal was to get more room nights booked. They monitored thousands of metrics, but they chose to define only one metric as a KPI. We call this example out because it is not the norm. Most of our clients have dozens, even hundreds, of KPIs.

30. At a 2015 interview in San Francisco, John Doerr shared an example in which OKRs were posted above the urinals in the men's bathroom! That may be a bit extreme, but it's one way to make OKRs visible.

31. While we've not conducted a formal study, anecdotal data indicates that limiting the ability to view OKRs to certain management levels is a more common practice in Europe than in the United States.

32. The same football example John Doerr once used to explain how OKRs cascade to Google many years ago appears on page 81 of his 2018 book, *Measure What Matters*. In 2015, Doerr clarified that "OKRs need not be hierarchically coupled." However, the football example reinforces the myth that OKRs are "tightly coupled."

33. Offer to help your OKRs project lead develop an OKRs FAQs document. A sample OKRs FAQs template is available to OKRs Coach Network members.

34. John Doerr told a story of how the CEO of Lotus – recall Lotus 123 – adopted OKRs and created "NOKRs." The "N" stands for "Not." Lotus used NOKRs to specify what they would not do: "Lotus should not do hardware." Some of our clients adopt the "NOKR" concept to help communicate what they are choosing to *not* focus on.

CHAPTER 3 EXERCISE: **DEVELOP AN OKRs FAQs DOCUMENT**

Keep answers brief. Effective FAQs documents are at most 10 pages.
Be sure to:

- Explain why the organization is deploying OKRs.
- Address all 10 universal deployment parameters.
- Incorporate other deployment parameters to capture nuances.

CHAPTER FOUR

Playbook for Phase 2 – Training

By the end of this chapter, you will be able to . . .

- Distinguish between the three types of OKRs training workshops.
- Develop agendas for each type of training workshop.
- Create training materials based on your client's deployment parameters.

CHAPTER 3 ANALYZED DEPLOYMENT PARAMETERS in detail for a reason. You and your client may be tempted to begin your OKRs engagement with a training workshop to get started drafting OKRs. You might make the same mistake I made in Paris as detailed at the beginning of Chapter 3. Don't make this mistake. Instead, begin your engagement with a few deployment coaching sessions to align on each parameter. While agreeing on these parameters serves as the foundation for a successful OKRs training workshop, there is more to be done.

Here are seven questions that coaches often ask when preparing for workshops: (1) What are the types of OKRs training workshops? (2) Can you share an actual agenda from an onsite training workshop? (3) How can I best deliver remote training? (4) Who should attend? (5) What interactive exercises work best, and how do I facilitate them? (6) What prereading or homework do I advise my client to complete in advance? (7) What materials do I need to create and deliver to my client? This chapter answers these questions and more.

 ## BEGIN WITH INTRODUCTIONS AND CONTEXT

Let key members of your audience introduce themselves before diving into your training content. Participants tend to be more engaged when they get to speak first, plus you get the added logistical advantage that latecomers will not miss critical information if they arrive midway through introductions. Thus, you can insist that the workshop gets started five minutes past the planned start time rather than waiting, uncomfortably, for every single participant to arrive.

We find two-minute introductions work best. Each participant states their name, tenure, title, and how they feel OKRs can benefit the overall organization and their specific team. Invite anyone who has experience with OKRs in the past to comment on what worked well, and not so well. We advise having the executive sponsor, or whoever is the most senior person in the room, welcome everyone to the workshop and provide context. This opening summarizes why the organization is deploying OKRs and any ground rules (e.g., turn off mobile phones) during the workshop. Next, introduce yourself and present the agenda for the workshop on a single slide with two parts: (1) theory and (2) application. If your client has already started with OKRs, provide a brief assessment of what's working well along with areas for improvement.[1]

THEORY AND APPLICATION: THE TWO PARTS OF AN OKRs TRAINING WORKSHOP

The first part, *theory*, is relatively short and features you doing most of the talking. The second part, *application*, is an interactive workshop that gets everyone applying theory and often includes breakout groups.

Training Part 1: Theory

Theory begins with an overview of OKRs and concludes with a section summarizing how your client is deploying OKRs. We often start the overview with a slide that details why organizations deploy OKRs in general, followed by an interactive discussion to confirm why your client has decided to roll out OKRs. This allows you to build off the executive sponsor's opening remarks and reinforces your client's goals for their OKRs program.

The overview covers: (1) the history and definition of OKRs, (2) examples of what OKRs *are* and what OKRs *are not*, and (3) tips for avoiding common pitfalls at each step of the OKRs cycle.[2] Overviews are more engaging when they emphasize areas critical to your specific client's situation. For example, if your client is considering setting OKRs at the individual level, include a slide summarizing the pros and cons of setting OKRs at the individual level. Similarly, if you have a client concerned about how KPIs work with OKRs, include a slide comparing key results with KPIs.[3]

Incorporate brief interactive exercises to engage workshop participants throughout the overview. Audiences tend to drift after 15 minutes in lecture mode. Two interactions that work well include (1) distinguishing between a key result and a health metric and (2) asking how to make a poorly written OKR better. A sample exercise to help your client distinguish between a key result and a health metric is shown in Figure 4.1.[4]

Exercise: Distinguish between a health metric and a key result

Key Result: Near-term focus for measurable improvement

Example: _____

Health Metric: Metric to continue monitoring, but not the focus for immediate improvement

Example: _____

FIGURE 4.1   Sample exercise from an OKRs workshop to engage your participants

Instructions for Sample Workshop Exercise
- Present a slide like the one shown in Figure 4.1.
- Ask participants to share several metrics that they are currently tracking.
- Classify each metric as a health metric or a key result.
- Duration: 5–10 minutes.
- Key points to reinforce:
  - Just because you measure it, does not mean it is a key result.
  - Health metrics often take priority over key results if they move out of their "healthy range."
  - A given metric may shift from a key result to a health metric over time and vice versa.

The theory section concludes with an analysis of your client's deployment parameters to align on how your client will deploy OKRs. We often present each deployment parameter on its own slide. As you review each parameter, reinforce the concepts introduced in the overview that are most critical for your client's success. For example, after introducing the importance of starting with a small set of OKRs, you might share your client's decision to limit each team to a single objective to start.

Most deployment parameters are simply announced at the training. However, we recommend checking with your executive sponsor and project leads to identify one or two deployment parameters to present as open questions for input during the training. Even just presenting one parameter as an open item can help make your client's deployment section engaging. Once you've completed the theory, it's time for application. While theory is important, allocate most of your workshop time to application. Remember the OKRs coaching mantra: *The only way to learn OKRs is to do OKRs.*

Training Part 2: Application

There are three distinct types of OKRs workshops.[5] Each workshop features a set of desired outcomes and is intended for a certain audience. It is vital that you and your client align on the audience, duration, and goals before scheduling workshops. For onsite workshops, plan for at least two hours, ideally a full day. Remote workshops should be kept short. Our clients find remote workshops work best when limited to two to three hours. While there is no requirement that you complete each of these three applications in a specific order, they are presented in a typical sequence.

Application 1: Top-Level OKRs Workshop

Starting at the top provides context for lower-level OKRs. Include a select group of key leaders, including the CEO if possible. We recommend limiting the theory section to at most two hours. Leadership teams often want to start working on their OKRs within the first hour, so adjust the timing accordingly. When feasible, schedule this workshop as part of an existing planning retreat to review long-term strategy. A strategy review provides context for creating OKRs.

Goals of the Top-Level Workshop   All top-level OKRs workshops share the common goal of drafting an OKR. Most also have the goal of refining an OKR. Your client's deployment parameters inform how you structure the nuances of the workshop. For example, if you are using our recommended prescoring system, encourage your client to refine a key result that specifies the commit, target, and stretch. Most of our clients conduct a short preview or "dry run" of the training workshop with a few key participants including the executive sponsor to review open items.

For a full-day onsite workshop, you may have time to draft several OKRs and refine one or two. For a half-day onsite workshop, we advise you manage expectations by limiting the goal to drafting a single OKR and refining one key result. If you are facilitating a remote workshop, consider breaking this workshop into two separate sessions, each running roughly two hours. The goal of the first session is to introduce OKRs theory and begin drafting. The goal of the second session is to refine OKRs.

Sample Email with Prework for a Top-Level Workshop   Here is an actual email that an OKRs project lead sent to leadership to prepare for an upcoming top-level OKRs workshop. Use this sample as inspiration.

From: OKRs Project Lead
To: All Top-Level OKRs Workshop Participants
When: 1 week prior to workshop [send reminder 1-2 days before workshop]
Email Subject: Prep for OKRs Workshop
[Email Body]
Team,
Here is the required material to review ahead of our upcoming workshop on [date]:

- Pre-read: *Objectives and Key Results*, by Niven & Lamorte[6]
- Pre-watch: Christina Wodtke's Executioner's Tale[7]

Workshop Goal: Learn about the OKRs methodology and draft company-level OKRs in a workshop facilitated by [YOUR NAME], who is an expert on OKRs.

Preparation: Please submit an objective that you think is critical to focus on this year. Include a few sentences to explain why you feel the objective is important now. Company-level objectives should. . .

- Reflect overall business goals (not just your team).
- Begin with a verb (improve, increase, etc.).
- Be qualitative (no numbers).

Here are sample objectives as inspiration:[8]

Objective: Win Belgium market!

Why Now? Competitor X just closed three major accounts in Belgium, and while we continue to be the leader in the Netherlands, we are at risk of losing traction in Belgium. Belgium is a critical region for us to dominate, as it is home to many fashion trendsetters and key influencers.

Objective: Successfully launch add-on product ABC.

Why Now? With more than 1,000 of our customers validating their interest in product ABC with 20 key beta testers providing highly positive feedback, now is the time to launch product ABC as an add-on. It also further separates us from competitor X.

Objective: Win more big accounts to accelerate growth.

Why Now? Our company was built on small business. However, we've proven that we can implement new jobs for large customers and do it well. We won our largest account in 2020. Then in 2021, we won an even bigger one. Both accounts gave us satisfaction scores above 90%. Best of all, winning big deals expands the bonus pool for all staff!

We will compile the objectives you submit for review during the workshop. Please send these to me by replying to this email by [date].
Thanks,
[OKRS PROJECT LEAD NAME]

Sample Agenda for a Top-Level Workshop   If you can get a full day with leadership, take it. While a full day is ideal, an onsite top-level OKRs workshop should be planned for a minimum of four hours, one hour for theory and three for application. So, if you can only get a half-day with the leadership team, take the introductions and OKRs theory part of the agenda down to an hour. It is the application part of this workshop that is most valuable as it generates impactful conversations.

Here is a sample full-day agenda from an onsite top-level OKRs workshop:

Part 1 – Introductions/OKRs Theory
- 9:30–10:30 am: Introductions, CEO on why OKRs
- 10:30–11:15 am: OKRs 101 (benefits, definitions, examples, etc.)
- 15-minute break
- 11:30–noon: Our OKRs deployment plan
- Noon–1:00 pm: Lunch

Part 2 – OKRs Development/Application
- 1:00–2:00 pm: Group drafts key results for top-level objective
- 2:00–3:00 pm: Round 1 breakout to draft key results for an objective
- 3:00–4:00 pm: Report backs, feedback on draft key results
- 4:00–5:30 pm: Round 2 breakout and report back to refine key results
  - 45 minutes: Breakout groups refine key results
  - 45 minutes: Report backs, each group shares 1–2 improved key results
- 5:30–6:00 pm: Wrap-up – feedback, next steps, and key takeaways

Our client completed each item on this agenda and finished on time. However, this is not always the case. Top-level workshops often lead to conversations that reveal important topics no one anticipated. Therefore, you must be flexible. As the conversation evolves, check in several times with the executive sponsor throughout the day to ensure the workshop stays on track.

Unanticipated conversations may make it difficult to get through the planned agenda, and this may make you feel uncomfortable. However, top-level OKRs workshops are not about you getting through your agenda, they are about leadership using OKRs as a framework to have the right conversations. Here is a case study workshop that did not follow the planned agenda.

Case Study: ACME Homes Top-Level Workshop   I spent two days leading a top-level workshop with a home-building company. Let's refer to this company as "ACME Homes." Prior to the workshop, I had several deployment coaching sessions with the CEO and CFO. In addition to defining the agenda, we aligned on 12 deployment parameters and four candidate objectives to explore at the workshop. These objectives focused on (1) people, (2) customer, (3) growth, and (4) financial. Here are four parameters most relevant to this case study:

1. ***Level to set OKRs.*** Company level only to start.
2. ***Scoring key results.*** Stretch Target Commit with prescoring.
3. ***Cycle time.*** Annual objectives with quarterly key results.
4. ***Number of OKRs.*** Target three objectives, each with four key results.

Here is the planned agenda for this top-level workshop with ACME Homes:

Day 1 (Full Day)
- CEO/CFO Opening: strategic context and financial update (1 hour)
- Lecture: Introductions + OKRs theory (1 hour)
- Group: Draft key results for people objective + lunch (3 hours)
- Breakouts: Develop and share key results for customer objective (2 hours)

Day 2 (Half Day)
- Group: Refine customer and people OKRs (1 hour)
- Breakouts: Draft key results for growth objective (1 hour)
- Group: Finalize OKRs (2 hours)

While the first two hours followed the agenda, the actual ACME Homes workshop did not adhere to the planned agenda. Here is what actually occurred:

OKRs Workshop Day 1
Hour 1, CEO Opening. The CEO and CFO opened with an excellent summary of the strategy, market trends, and latest financials. The opening lasted an hour and was well received. Beginning with this leadership presentation set the stage for OKRs.

Hour 2, Introductions and OKRs Theory. Fifteen business leaders briefly introduced themselves, and we covered the theory of OKRs in about an hour. These first two hours matched the planned agenda perfectly.

Hours 3+, Group Exercise. Define Key Results for Objective 1: People. After the CEO introduced the people objective and why it was so important now, I facilitated a distributed learning workshop with the entire group.[9] Participants took five minutes to silently draft key results, five minutes to discuss in groups of two, and another five minutes to align on their top two key results to share with the entire group. Then, each small group presented their key results for discussion. This exercise always creates energy, as participants apply OKRs theory to practice. Here are some of the draft key results that emerged.

First Set of Draft Key Results
1. Increase % sales managers exceeding their target from X to Y.
2. Add X sales managers in Q4 with start date before January 1.
3. Baseline metric to reflect "sales manager engagement score."
4. Increase sales manager retention (excluding sales managers lost due to poor performance) with documented reasons why sales managers leave.

Action Plan[10]
1. Hire VP sales.
2. Train sales team.
3. Get more "A-players" on the sales team.

As we discussed ideas for key results and action plans from several groups, the energy in the room grew exponentially. I noticed that all proposed key results for the people objective revolved around the sales team.[11] Although we planned to let each breakout group articulate their key result candidates before going deeper and refining, one conversation seemed too important to interrupt.

As the CEO stared at the drafted key results and action plan on the white board, the room became quiet. Then, he announced his concern, "While we want sales managers to hit their targets, that's not enough to be an 'A-player.'" A member of the advisory board asked, "Who do we have on the sales team now that is an A-player?" To which the CEO replied, "Amy is definitely not an A-player. One big month where you blow out your target does not make you an

A-player. You need consistency, you need a good rating from your customers. Also, you need to collaborate effectively with various teams inside our company." We had our first break-through. It was time to pivot from the planned agenda.

The CEO's discussion with the board member resonated with the larger group. This conversation led to a key insight: We did not have a definition of what it meant to be an "A-player," and having such a definition would be critical to success going forward. The sentiment in the room was that most sales managers were not operating at an A-level. However, it was unrealistic to expect anyone to operate at an A-level if the leadership did not even know how to define the term.

With only an hour left for day one, we had to make the decision whether to move on to the next objective or keep working on this first objective. The CEO was decisive. He emphasized the importance of getting the first objective right before moving on to others. Thus, we kept focused on the first objective.

We planned to cover two objectives on day one, but we did not even complete the drafting process for the key results of the first objective! We did not end day one on track to begin drafting key results for the third objective on day two. I felt like we failed to make adequate progress at the end of that first day. I asked the CEO how he felt. The CEO looked me in the eyes and said, "Ben, I've been to over 20 corporate retreats like this, and this is one of the best in our company's history. We had the conversation we needed. We started to articulate the problem, that we lack a definition of what it means to be an A-player."[12] Thanks to the CEO, I slept well that night.

OKRs Workshop Day 2
We continued to define the characteristics of an "A-player" via brainstorm and arrived at the following definition in the form of a checklist.

Definition of an ACME Homes A-Player Sales Manager
1. Hit overall sales target on a rolling six-month average
2. Willingness to refer based on customer surveys at 90%+ as measured over the last three months, compared to our historical average of 87%
3. Trained on internal systems as measured by our internal systems team

4. Positive score on internal 360 review to reflect that you have a good attitude when interacting with our internal staff
5. Proactiveness and sales discipline as measured by creating three or more leads and adding them to Salesforce.com each month

The objective evolved from "People: Grow and retain a world-class staff with a focus on Sales" into "Position ACME Homes as a sales machine." Here is the refined OKR.

Q4 Objective: Position ACME to be a sales machine as we enter the new year.

Why Now? To meet growing housing demand, we plan to hire a record number of sales managers over the next six months. We have a proven process for defining sales targets, but it is not scalable. We cannot scale effectively when sales managers close deals and leave it for the rest of the organization to pick up the pieces. To be a sales machine, we must do more than expand the team and hit the numbers. We must agree on what it means for our sales managers to be "A-players" and put a system in place that enables all sales managers to become A-players.

Q4 Key Results:

1. Increase the percentage of sales managers exceeding target from 70% in Q3 to 90% in Q4.
2. Add 20 new sales managers in Q4 with start date before January 1.
3. Classify five test sales managers as A, B, or C players based on our new definitions of sales-manager performance levels. (Expectations: All sales managers employed 4+ months classified by end of Q1 next year, based on criteria we define in Q4.)

Coaching Takeaways for Top-Level OKRs Workshops

- ✔ Solicit objectives prior to top-level workshops.
- ✔ Conduct a workshop preview with your executive sponsor when feasible.
- ✔ Be flexible! If your client is having an important conversation, forget about the agenda and let them drive. In the ACME Homes case, the CEO took charge and got everyone thinking about what it means to be an "A-player."
- ✔ As key results emerge, revisit the objective. In the ACME Homes case study, drafting key results helped refine the objective from a broad concept around "people" to a more focused objective around becoming a "sales machine."
- ✔ *Less is more:* One fully baked OKR is often better than several half-baked ones.

Application 2: OKRs Expert Workshop

The OKRs expert workshop is designed to help your client develop the in-house capacity to sustain their OKRs program long after you are gone. It is especially valuable for organizations that are setting OKRs at the team level.

Goals of the Expert Workshop   Let's go back to how and why this workshop got started. In 2014, I co-created a full-day OKRs expert training with Zalando, one of my early clients.[13] Zalando asked me to train a group of 20 mid-level managers to become OKRs experts who could support the OKRs program in their respective business areas.

This first training represented a major milestone in my development as an OKRs coach. We were breaking into uncharted territory. To my knowledge, no external coaches offered a full-day OKRs expert training workshop back in 2014. The energy and insights coming out of our first OKRs expert training exceeded our expectations. Zalando asked me to return to Europe to facilitate more workshops.

The Zalando team and I developed a systematic approach to training coaches to support an OKRs program at scale. Unlike the top-level workshop that focuses on drafting real OKRs, the expert workshop focuses on developing OKRs coaching skills. Anyone at Zalando completing the OKRs expert training workshop was invited to take on a new role that we named *internal OKRs coach*.

To be classified as an internal OKRs coach at Zalando required three steps:

1. Complete the OKRs expert training day.
2. Facilitate an OKRs drafting workshop with a team.
3. Attend an end-of-the-quarter retrospective and share a learning with other internal OKRs coaches.

The majority of expert training participants became internal OKRs coaches.

Building off the success of the OKRs expert workshop developed with Zalando, we started offering it to other organizations.[14] As with all OKRs workshops, the key to success with the expert workshop is to allocate most of the time to application. Remember the mantra, *the only way to learn OKRs is to do OKRs*. And for the OKRs expert training, small breakout groups work best.

Breaking out into groups of three to four participants is the essential feature of the expert workshop. Each breakout team has three roles: (1) coach, (2) coachee, and (3) observer. The coach asks questions to help the coachee draft their OKRs; observers listen and take notes without interrupting. Observers write down coaching questions that lead to break-throughs and questions they wish the coach had asked their coachee. The focus is on gaining the skills to be an OKRs coach rather than making progress defining actual OKRs. We advise completing two breakout rounds, so that everyone gets a chance to play the role of coach or coachee.

Onsite delivery ranges from six to eight hours.[15] We advise allowing a full hour for the first breakout round. For the second breakout, keep the groups the same but have each group member play a different role. If pressed for time, consider a rapid 30-minute breakout for round two, as illustrated in the sample agenda below.

Sample Agenda for an Onsite OKRs Expert Workshop
- 9:00–9:30 am: Welcome and introductions
- 9:30–10:00 am: OKRs theory
- 10:00–10:45 am: Group exercise: Draft key results for a top-level OKR
- 10:45–11:00 am: Break
- 11:00–11:30 am: Creating team-level OKRs in seven steps
- 11:30–12:30 pm: Breakout round 1: A coaches B, C observes
- 12:30–1:30 pm: Lunch
- 1:30–2:00 pm: Share backs
- 2:00–2:30 pm: Rapid breakout round 2: B coaches C, A observes
- 2:30–3:00 pm: Share backs
- 3:00–3:30 pm: Wrap-up: feedback, next steps, and key takeaways

Participants in OKRs Expert Workshops Expert workshops are best delivered onsite with 12 to 18 participants.[16] We find that the energy level decreases below 12 people and loses intimacy beyond 18. For larger groups, consider expanding some breakout groups to include four instead of three participants. We recommend limiting onsite workshops to at most 24 participants, as this group can be broken out into six groups of four. In a group of four, the additional group member plays an observer role. Thus, groups of four consist of one coach, one coachee, and two observers. While the size of the workshop matters, it is even more critical to include a diverse group of participants in expert training workshops.

Coaching works best when the coach and the coachee are from different functional teams. We advise you assign each member of a given functional team to a unique breakout group. For example, a member of the finance team might coach someone from the engineering team. This requires the engineer to use plain language rather than technical jargon. Coaches from different domains tend to ask clarifying questions. They help their coachee use language that people outside of the coachee's team can understand.

In addition to the prework recommended in the sample email for the top-level workshop, this field book is an excellent resource for anyone attending the expert workshop. Sample materials for the expert workshop detailing the questions coaches ask during each breakout are available to members of the OKRs Coach Network.[17]

Coaching Takeaways for OKRs Expert Workshops

✔ Offer this workshop to organizations looking to develop internal OKRs coaches.
✔ Define three roles for breakouts: (1) coach, (2) coachee, and (3) observer.
✔ Design breakout groups with three to four participants from distinct teams.

Application 3: Team-Level OKRs Workshop

Team-level workshops have two prerequisites. First, you must agree on the "teams" that will set OKRs so you know who to include in the workshop. Second, some form of top-level OKRs must be in place. Team members often complain that they cannot create OKRs for their team without top-level OKRs as context. For this reason, we advise you to begin team-level workshops with a presentation of top-level OKRs, ideally by a senior executive.[18]

Goals of the Team-Level Workshop   All team-level workshops share the common goal of drafting OKRs at the team level. Some team-level workshops may also focus on refining OKRs. Here is a sample set of goals for a team-level workshop developed with one of our clients:

■ Three teams draft a mission, objective/why, and at least two key results.
■ All participants document how a short-term key result connects to top-level strategy or horizontally to a dependent team's goals.
■ All participants document a key takeaway to apply at work.

Participants in a Team-Level Workshop   Before you can determine who to include in team-level workshops, you and your client must agree on the teams that define OKRs.[19] Our early clients often requested separate workshops for each team. While this approach worked in some cases, it was often counterproductive, especially when introducing functional teams to OKRs. One of our clients planned a workshop day as follows: two-hour workshop with the customer success team, two-hour workshop with the finance team, two-hour workshop with the sales team, and so on. Because each functional team setting OKRs already worked in silos, this approach inadvertently increased silo effects.

While it can be challenging to include team members from multiple functional teams in a workshop, we recommend taking on this challenge. Our clients report that their team-level OKRs workshops are more effective when they involve members from several functional teams right from the start. We recommend including representation from three to five functional teams in each workshop.[20]

Sample Agenda for a Team-Level Workshop   We often use the "mass connect" approach for running team-level OKRs workshops with multiple teams.[21] Here is a sample agenda that we used with one of our clients:

- 8:00–9:00 am: Introductions, CEO briefing on OKRs journey
- 9:00–10:00 am: OKRs theory/refresher and review of top-level OKRs
- 10:00–11:00 am: Draft team-level OKRs
- 11:00–12:00 pm: Report backs and idea sharing
- 12:00–1:00 pm: Lunch
- 1:00–2:00 pm: Refine OKRs, participants interact outside their team to align on dependencies
- 2:00–2:45 pm: Report backs
- 2:45–3:00 pm: Next steps and key takeaways

Coaching Takeaways for Team-Level Workshops

- ✔ Schedule team-level workshops *after* defining OKRs teams.
- ✔ Include members from multiple functional teams to foster cross-functional alignment.
- ✔ Begin with an overview of top-level OKRs to create context.

Customizing OKRs Training Workshops

Once you master these three application workshops, consider incorporating various elements to design a customized training plan that is ideal for your client. For example, one of our clients wanted to complete all three application workshops in just two days and train all executives and their direct reports. So, for day one with executives, we tested out the idea of a top-level workshop in the morning, followed by a three-person breakout round from the expert workshop in the afternoon. This approach enabled each executive to draft top-level OKRs while also developing their OKRs coaching skills. This also provided the initial top-level OKRs that served as context for day two with leadership's direct reports.

Day two kicked off with our standard OKRs expert workshop breakouts. However, we positioned it as a team-level OKRs drafting workshop. In other words, instead of the mass-connect approach that begins by breaking out by team, we defined breakout groups comprised of three members from different teams. The team-level OKRs emerging from these small expert workshop breakouts were then used as drafts for team-level OKRs. We completed all three application workshops and trained executives and their direct in just two days![22]

 NOTES

1. Sample assessment models are available to members of the OKRs Coach Network.
2. Refer to Chapter 5 for an analysis of how to avoid common pitfalls at each step of the OKRs cycle.
3. Refer to the table comparing key results to KPIs in Figure 3.5 for inspiration.
4. Consider creating a slide for your training deck based on "Examples of Ineffective and Effective Key Results," as illustrated in Figure E.1 from the Epilogue. Additional exercises are available to OKRs Coach Network members.
5. While we define three types of OKRs workshops in this book, some organizations request training specifically for key result champions. However, we do not consider this to be a training workshop as it requires just one hour. In this session, we review the key result champion role, create a sample action plan for a key result, and answer questions.
6. Chapter 1 of *Objectives and Key Results* can be downloaded for free via OKRs.com as a PDF.
7. You may choose any video. We include Christina's 21-minute video because it is brief and engaging: https://vimeo.com/86392023.
8. Use these objectives as examples or incorporate your own. While we presented three in this email, advise your client to include just one or two objectives that are relevant to their industry.

9. I witnessed the effectiveness of the distributed learning approach for facilitating workshops as part of a graduate student course through Stanford's Center for Teaching and Learning in the late 1990s. Here's a valuable tip to maintaining engagement and keeping the energy level high: End each 5-minute group discussion right when the energy is peaking. In other words, don't go by the clock, go by the energy level; this is typically 3–6 minutes, depending on the group dynamic.

10. Some of our clients like to add an "action plan" section below each OKR to brainstorm key action items that they believe will impact the given OKR.

11. As key results emerge, the objective often changes. The importance of taking an iterative approach is covered in Chapter 5. Refer to Figure 5.2 for a visual.

12. Getting into a valuable conversation is an indicator the workshop is going well. After all, OKRs is a critical thinking framework that helps teams to align on problems to solve. Jeff Walker, my original OKRs mentor, often told me, "If you understand the problem, it's easy to solve. The problem is that we spend too much time trying to solve the problem rather than taking the time to clearly define it."

13. Zalando is an e-commerce company based in Berlin. For more on Zalando and its OKRs program, refer to the case study interview included in Chapter 7 of *Objectives and Key Results: Driving Focus, Alignment, and Engagement* by Niven and Lamorte, Wiley, 2016. My contacts at Zalando report that OKRs continue to be used with great success.

14. Some of our clients refer to "OKRs Expert Training" as "OKRs Ambassador Training" or "Train the Trainer." Use whatever name works best for you and your client.

15. The remote equivalent is best delivered over two or three sessions. Each session runs two to three hours.

16. We recently discovered that expert workshops can also be delivered remotely leveraging breakout room functionality. In fact, we have had success with groups of up to fifty. However, we find it best to limit this remote training to a single session of at most three hours. If you deliver this workshop remotely, define remote breakout groups of four (or even five) to mitigate potential issues due to internet connectivity. You do not want a breakout group room with a single person, given that this exercise requires a coaching dialog with at least two participants.

17. You may also develop training materials for expert workshops based on the Questions OKRs Coaches Ask in the Epilogue.

18. If top-level OKRs are not finalized, the executive sponsor may share a draft of top-level OKRs. If your client chooses not to define top-level OKRs, the executive sponsor often presents a strategic overview as context for drafting team-level OKRs.

19. Refer to the first deployment parameter in Chapter 3 for an analysis of how to define the teams that will set OKRs.

20. The guidance to include multiple teams is especially important when setting OKRs with functional teams. When creating OKRs for cross-functional squads or pods that already include team members from various functions, it often works well to define team-level OKRs with a single squad or pod.

21. For more on the "mass connect" approach, refer to page 106 of *Objectives and Key Results: Driving Focus, Alignment, and Engagement* by Niven and Lamorte, Wiley, 2016.
22. Several OKRs coaches, including me, find the three-person breakout approach as outlined in the expert training workshop to be the most effective and rewarding approach to getting up to speed on OKRs. To this end, we now advise that our coaches include the three-person breakout exercise when defining team-level OKRs.
23. Refer to the sample handout in the Epilogue as inspiration.

CHAPTER 4 EXERCISE: **DESIGN AN OKRs WORKSHOP**

Your workshop design should include:

- Detailed agenda, goals, and participants
- Email to announce the training
- Slide deck (10–30 slides)
- Handout (1–4 pages)[23]

Playbook for Phase 3 – Cycle Coaching

By the end of this chapter, you will be able to . . .

- Coach your client through all three steps in an OKRs cycle.
- Avoid common pitfalls at each step.
- Design an OKRs tracker for your client to use at each step.
- Create OKRs coaching emails.

M Y FATHER, MARIO LAMORTE, was a master elementary schoolteacher. In his freewriting exercise, he provided simple instructions: write down whatever is on your mind while keeping your pencil moving for 10 minutes. One gloomy student approached him with a sad look and complained, "I can't think of anything to write – it's frustrating to see the other kids writing so fast." My father replied, "Perfect! Write down exactly what you just told me. You're off to a great start." The student returned to her desk and started writing. While Mario's freewriting workshop generated enthusiasm, the real work was just beginning.

My father took the journals home to read over the weekend and inserted personal notes, questions, and encouraging comments. He created an ongoing dialog and collaborative relationship with each student. His approach to teaching writing informs my approach to OKRs coaching.

The training described in Chapter 4 generates enthusiasm. If you are an OKRs trainer, you might simply deliver training and move on to your next project. But you are not a trainer. You are a coach.

Like my father with his students, you know the workshop is just the beginning of an ongoing collaboration. You provide coaching throughout the OKRs cycle to ensure your client translates theory into practice. While your client may not have a journal, they often provide written OKRs for your feedback. Your encouraging comments and questions enable the ongoing collaboration that is essential to OKRs coaching.

This chapter breaks down how to coach your client through the steps of an OKRs cycle. Each step begins with solutions for avoiding common pitfalls. To make this concrete, we include excerpts from actual cycle coaching sessions and a case study that follows one of our client's OKRs through each step of the cycle.

 ## STEP 1: SET AND ALIGN OKRs

Pitfalls
- Defining too many OKRs
- Writing key results as a list of tasks, measuring output not outcomes
- Failing to define why the objective is important now
- Creating OKRs in silos, ignoring dependencies

Solutions
- Focus on one to three objectives per team.
- Distinguish between key results, health metrics, and tasks.
- Align on why each objective is important prior to drafting key results.
- Involve key stakeholders outside your team when drafting OKRs.

Most organizations that approach us have already tried to roll out OKRs on their own. They often want to use OKRs to focus, but define way too many OKRs. We were recently approached by a team that defined 11 objectives! They presented us with a massive list of key results that looked more like tasks than measurable outcomes. Some organizations seek to use OKRs to increase cross-functional alignment and reduce silo effects. Ironically, these same organizations often define teams based on their org chart and ask each team to draft OKRs in silos.

When approached by a prospective client that has encountered these pitfalls, let them know they are not alone. Provide validation. Remind your prospective client that it takes time to get OKRs right. Present them with the solutions outlined in this book, and they may go on to become your client. To help your client avoid these pitfalls and define effective OKRs, we designed the seven steps for creating team-level OKRs, shown in Figure 5.1.

Seven Steps for Creating Team-Level OKRs

1 **Agree on a Mission**

2 **Check Alignment**

3 **Develop Objectives** *(Why Now?)*

4 **Draft Key Results**

5 **Convert Tasks to Key Results**

6 **Challenge the Set of Key Results**

7 **Refine Key Results. Finalize Team-Level OKRs**

FIGURE 5.1 The seven steps for creating team-level OKRs

While the first two steps, mission and alignment check, are not technically part of defining OKRs, do not skip them. These first two steps create valuable context for drafting team-level OKRs. Here is a sample OKR we developed with a client after completing these seven steps with a marketing team:

Marketing Team Mission: Provide tools to enable our sales team to sell and beat the competition.

Alignment Check: We depend on sales, product, and customer success. Sales and finance depend on us.

Objective: Increase the quality of leads, cost effectively.

Why Now? We are not measuring the return on investment (ROI) of major marketing spend at events, and our new CEO wants visibility now to create an ROI-based marketing plan next year. Cost per lead at $105 is not viable as we scale and is a key driver in the financial plan. The sales team reports that the quality of leads we deliver is poor.

Key Results:

1. Obtain baseline ROI of marketing as measured by reporting revenue/cost for 5 conferences where we spent $50,000 or more.
2. Reduce overall cost per lead from $105 in Q4 to $75 in Q1.
3. Double the quality of leads as measured by an increase in leads that convert to opportunity within six weeks of creation from 20% to 40%.

This section breaks down the steps we took to develop this sample OKR. The steps are meant to be iterative. For example, our clients often return to Step 3 to revisit their objective after working on key results in later steps as shown in Figure 5.2. Our analysis of each step includes questions to ask and tips for success.

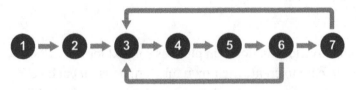

FIGURE 5.2 Common iterations back to step 3, develop objectives

1. Agree on a Mission

Many organizations implement OKRs to shorten their planning cycle. Shorter cycles create more opportunities to adjust course. However, introducing short cycles can also be a potential pitfall of OKRs. Are OKRs too shortsighted? How can OKRs be strategic if they look out only for three months? How can we ensure that each team's OKRs are connected to a longer-term mission?

Here is a simple equation to connect OKRs to a longer-term mission: M + OKRs = MOKRs where "M" stands for "mission."[1] Most organizations define company-level missions. If your client does not have a company-level mission in place, put the OKRs program on hold and complete a mission exercise with your client's leadership team right away. A company-level mission is the foundation upon which to build OKRs.[2] As most organizations do not define missions at the team level, you have an opportunity to add value right away.

We recommend starting with missions with every team you coach. Team-level missions provide context for drafting OKRs and help connect work to the bigger picture. Our clients consistently report that developing team-level missions is time well spent. We advise teams to allocate one hour each year to refresh their missions. Figure 5.3 summarizes the mission statement exercise that we use with our clients.

Here is the outcome of Step 1 from our sample marketing team.

Marketing Team Mission: Provide tools to enable our sales team to sell and beat the competition.

Three Questions to Ask:
1. In one sentence, how would you describe your team's purpose?
2. Whom do we serve?
3. What service do we offer?

Tips
- Confirm a companywide mission is in place as context for all OKRs.
- Encourage each team to create their own mission; revisit it each year.
- Provide your client with a simple mission exercise like the one in Figure 5.3.

Mission Exercise Overview

Purpose	Define team-level missions.
Attendees	All team members; ideally a small group of at most 12
Duration	One hour
Mission Sentence	Your team's mission sentence should be a single sentence that answers the questions: • Why do we exist? • Whom do we serve? • What do we offer? • What is the long-term impact we make?
Step-by-Step Instructions	1. Each team member takes a few minutes to write down what they feel is the team's mission. 2. Team members compare their mission sentences in groups of two. 3. Each group of two presents their best mission sentence. 4. A facilitator captures keywords that resonate with the team as they emerge.

FIGURE 5.3   Sample mission exercise

2. Check Alignment

Amazing outcomes almost always require collaboration across teams. Some organizations create cross-functional squads. Others define team-level OKRs based on their org chart.[3] Regardless of how OKRs teams are defined, take time at the beginning of each OKRs cycle to identify near-term dependencies across teams. If a given team has a strong dependency on another team, consider including key stakeholders from outside the team. Input from outside the team often leads to a dependent key result or a shared OKR and can improve cross-functional alignment.[4]

We are often tempted to skip the alignment check. However, our clients find it useful to take 5 to 10 minutes to identify dependencies outside their team before diving into OKRs. While several minutes is sufficient for most teams, other teams allocate more time for this step.[5] Here is the outcome of Step 2 from our sample marketing team.

We depend on . . .
- Product to design features and new products.
- Sales to call new leads and provide feedback when we lose.
- Customer success to create happy customers that agree to be featured in marketing collateral.

These teams depend on us . . .
- Sales team needs us to provide leads.
- Finance team needs us to report ROI and minimize cost per lead.

Three Questions to Ask:
1. Which teams do your objectives depend on?
2. Which teams do you collaborate with most often?
3. Which teams depend on you? How?

Tips
- If there is a critical dependency on another team in the upcoming OKRs cycle, consider creating a shared OKR.
- While five minutes may suffice to check alignment, allow more time for highly engaged clients.

3. Develop Objectives (Why Now?)

After checking alignment, your client is ready to draft objectives. We recommend reviewing top-level OKRs as context for creating team-level OKRs. However, creating team-level objectives requires critical thinking. Avoid the direct cascade approach, as outlined in Chapter 3. Teams should not copy and paste higher-level key results to define their team's objectives.

While the creative process of developing objectives is more of an art than a science, our clients do best with some guidance. We advise the following three guidelines to help your clients develop objectives: (1) Write as a single sentence, (2) Begin with a verb, and (3) Define a focus area for improvement, not maintenance. We also advise presenting one or two sample objectives that are relevant to your client.[6] Here are three sample objectives, followed by a short paragraph detailing why each objective is important now.

Objective: Improve our onboarding process with a focus on engineers.
Why Now? We are now onboarding more than 50 engineers each month. While our onboarding process worked well a few years ago when we were growing slowly, employee feedback from the last two quarters makes it clear that we need a more efficient and consistent process. While some engineers report our onboarding process is acceptable, nearly 40% report that it did not meet their expectations. Given we expect to be at a run rate of nearly 100 engineers per month by end of year, now is the time to optimize our onboarding process.
Objective: Create a culture of cybersecurity readiness.
Why Now? After losing Nikita and Rajesh, we are now a small team of fewer than 10. With these losses, Denny is the only team member we have certified in several critical areas. Now is the time to get our team trained so we have at least two team members (not just Denny) able to resolve security issues in all 15 critical areas.
Objective: Figure out where the money we make comes from.
Why Now? We can close the books each month and produce accurate financial reports. However, we do not have enough visibility into revenue by channel with 45% of revenue classified as "OTHER" last year. Our CEO joked that if we could just increase "OTHER" by 10%, we'd hit our financial goals. Once we identify the sources of revenue, we can develop a more realistic plan for increasing revenue.

After presenting examples of objectives and why they are important now, give teams 15 to 30 minutes to draft one objective with three to five sentences that explain why their objective is so important right now. The explanation of "Why now?" should educate and motivate staff. Be sure to specify how the objective connects to higher-level goals (vertical alignment) or to another team's goals (horizontal alignment). Our sample marketing team's objective has both vertical and horizontal connections, as "cost effectively" connects vertically to the company's profitability goal and "quality of leads" connects horizontally to sales team goals. Here is the outcome of the objective exercise for our sample marketing team.

Objective: Increase the quality of leads, cost effectively.
Why Now? We are not measuring the return on investment (ROI) of major marketing spend at events, and our new CEO wants visibility now to create an ROI-based marketing plan next year. Cost per lead at $105 is not viable as we scale and is a key driver in the financial plan. The sales team reports that the quality of leads we deliver is poor.

Three Questions to Ask:

1. *Fundamental objective question:* What is the most important area to focus on making measurable progress in the near term?
2. Why is this objective so important now?
3. If the team had to focus on a single objective, what would it be?

Tips

- When struggling to define objectives, consider going back to Step 1 to revisit the team mission.
- Do not copy top-level key results and paste them as team-level objectives.
- Include several sentences that answer the question: "Why is the objective so important now?"
- In addition to educating and motivating staff, the explanation of "Why now?" should clarify how the objective is aligned (i.e., vertically to higher-level goals or horizontally to other teams.)

4. Draft Key Results

Objectives tend to be easy to draft. Key results tend to be difficult to write as precise, measurable statements. The best way to master this step, and the remaining steps that cover how to finalize key results, is to review excerpts from coaching conversations and reflect on your own sessions. Specifically, we recommend reflecting on your actual OKRs coaching sessions multiple times using the left-hand column exercise detailed at the end of Chapter 1.

Sample draft key results that represent the outcome of this fourth step with our sample marketing team include: (1) reduce cost of leads from X to Y, (2) remove leads with personal email addresses from qualified leads, and (3) estimate the cost of marketing events.

Three Questions to Ask:

1. *Fundamental key result question:* At the end of the period, how will we know "the objective" will be achieved?
2. What metric needs to move to reflect progress on the objective?
3. How will we make the objective measurable?

Tips

- Give your client time to write silently when drafting key results. Ask each participant to write as many ideas as possible in a few minutes. Then, have them compare their draft key results in groups of two and share their best key result.

- Specify the baseline! Instead of writing a key result in the form "Increase metric A to Y," specify the baseline so that the key result takes the form of "Increase metric A from X to Y." If the current value is unknown, encourage your client to explore a baseline key result.

- Focus on the essence of key results when drafting. Do not obsess on the exact values of X and Y at this stage. You can use an approximation, so that the draft key result takes the form of "Increase metric A from $\sim X$ to $\sim Y$."

5. Convert Tasks to Key Results

When drafting key results for an objective, one often produces a list of tasks. Coming up with a to-do list is perfectly fine, but remember, tasks are not key results. Teams must convert these tasks into key results or remove tasks from the list of potential key results altogether.

Let's look at how one of our sample marketing team's draft key results was converted from a task to a key result. The draft key result, "Remove leads with personal email addresses from qualified leads," is a task. Our client reported that removing leads with personal email addresses like "@yahoo.com" or @gmail.com" could be done by a single person within a week. After coaching, this task was converted to a result that reflected the intended outcome to "increase conversion from X to Y as measured by the percentage of leads that convert to opportunity within six weeks of creation."

Three Questions to Ask:

1. **_Fundamental task-to-key result question:_** What is the intended outcome of the task?
2. If we complete the task, does that mean we've achieved the objective?
3. What is the best possible outcome you can imagine that could result from completing the task?

Tips

- Remind your client that it's important that each key result has an action plan, but that these action items need not be listed as key results.
- To ensure your client feels heard, consider creating a list of tasks below the OKRs drafting document. For example, several of our clients call their critical task list "Just Do Its!"
- Explain that the list of "Just Do Its!" can include activities that consume significant team resources. A given action item may drive a health metric or key result or reflect a high-priority compliance activity that just needs to get done (e.g., "complete the audit" or "update security software").

6. Challenge the Set of Key Results

Key results should be complementary. They should represent the minimal set of important metrics required to define the achievement of an objective. If an objective has three key results that are all highly correlated, the overall set of key results may be redundant. Each key result should add value. A good set of key results work together to tell different parts of the objective story.

Teams that use OKRs effectively often have complementary key results that reflect quantity and quality. Two key results that illustrate how our sample marketing team drafted both a quantity and a quality key result for their objective are:

1. **Quantity key result.** Increase inbound leads from 500 to 1,000.
2. **Quality key result.** Increase conversion from 20% to 40% as measured by leads that convert to opportunity within six weeks of creation.

If the team focuses only on the *quantity* key result to get more leads, they might find a decrease in the *quality* of leads. By including both key results, the team can focus on both lead quantity and lead quality. In addition to balancing quantity and quality, teams that use OKRs effectively often define a set of key results that include both leading and lagging indicators.

Leading indicators tend to be more controllable and are often referred to as *inputs*. Lagging indicators tend to be classified as *outputs* and may not be very controllable, especially in the near term. Examples of lagging indicators include bottom-line metrics such as revenue, profit, and average revenue per employee. Examples of leading indicators include metrics such as new leads created, website traffic, and landing page conversion rates. Here's an example that illustrates how our sample marketing team might balance leading and lagging indicators:

> **_Leading indicator key result:_** Increase conversion rate on landing pages from 3% to 5%.
> **_Lagging indicator key result:_** Increase marketing contribution to pipeline from $1.5 million to $2 million.

In this case, marketing feels like they can get to work right away, testing to optimize landing page conversion rates. However, it will take time, possibly several months, before this increased conversion rate impacts the pipeline. Because increasing landing page conversion rate drives an increase in pipeline, landing page conversion is the leading indicator, or input, and pipeline is the lagging indicator, or output.[7]

Three Questions to Ask:
1. If all key results are achieved, is the objective also achieved?
2. How can the set of key results be reduced?
3. Do the key results capture quantity and quality? Leading and lagging?

Tips
- If a given objective has several key results that appear to be highly correlated, eliminate at least one key result. Apply the _less is more_ mantra!
- Look for a balanced set of key results that include both quality and quantity as well as a mix of leading and lagging indicators.
- As the set of key results evolves, revisit the objective. The seven steps are not meant to be perfectly sequential. Remember to iterate as illustrated in Figure 5.2.

7. Refine Key Results. Finalize Team-Level OKRs.

Prior to publishing OKRs, use the characteristics of effective key results as a checklist to further refine key results. The eight characteristics of key results are:

1. **_"Key," not "all."_** Will the key result inspire action that will move the needle, or does it reflect business-as-usual maintenance work?
2. **_Specific._** Use specific language to avoid ambiguity.
3. **_Measurable._** Progress should not be subject to opinion.
4. **_Results, not tasks._** Key results are results/outcomes, not tasks.

5. *Clear.* Use high school English with only standard acronyms.
6. *Aspirational.* You achieve more when you set the bar high.
7. *Scored.* Use confidence scores to manage expectations.
8. *Champion.* Each key result has a champion who updates progress and ensures the key result does not slip through the cracks.

Once key results are refined, some of our clients publish their OKRs. However, some organizations that define OKRs at the team level prefer to conduct one final review to ensure alignment prior to publishing. Assuming that your client included input from dependent teams when drafting OKRs, your client's OKRs are likely horizontally aligned. However, in addition to horizontal validation across teams, team-level OKRs should be vertically validated.

We recommend team leads share their OKRs with senior leadership for final approval just before publishing to confirm vertical alignment. Consider facilitating brief conversations between team leads and leadership. Once OKRs are approved, ensure your client publishes OKRs in a single location. We call this single location *the OKRs tracker*. Dikran Yapoujian, the first certified coach to join the OKRs.com team, discovered an excellent way to introduce a client to the OKRs tracker.

CONTRIBUTION: **MAKE A GOOD FIRST IMPRESSION WITH THE OKRs TRACKER**

Dikran Yapoujian, first OKRs.com certified coach

When I first started with Ben in 2018, I sent a generic OKRs tracker spreadsheet to my client early in the engagement. The tracker was often loaded with one of their draft OKRs from a training workshop. I noticed that many of these clients did not fully integrate the OKRs tracker into their workflow. As an experiment with one of my clients, I loaded all their initial OKRs into the tracker. When I introduced the tracker with their OKRs populated, my client was blown away. The enthusiasm was palpable. We could easily identify what was missing once we had OKRs organized in a standard template.

While I present the generic OKRs tracker as part of deployment coaching, I deliver the tracker populated with the OKRs from their training workshop to set the stage for their first cycle. The tracker ensures they ask the right questions about each key result to drive value at each step of the cycle. Adoption is amazing. My clients now start team meetings with a review of their OKRs tracker and are focused on the right questions.

Three Questions to Ask:

1. ***"Key," not "all."*** Is this a focus for improvement now or is it already in an acceptable range?
2. ***Measurable.*** Rather than writing the key result as "Increase metric A to Y," can it be written as "Increase metric A from X to Y?" What is the baseline?
3. ***Scored.*** What is a commit level of progress within our team's control that feels 90% likely to be achieved? What is a stretch outcome that represents a 10% confidence level?

Tips

- Use the characteristics of effective key results when refining key results.
- Consider reviewing OKRs with leadership to confirm vertical alignment.
- Load final OKRs into a single location to ensure visibility throughout the cycle.

STEP 2: CHECK IN AND MONITOR

Pitfalls

- Zero OKRs review – "set-it-and-forget-it"
- Too many OKRs-specific meetings and processes

Solutions

- Conduct a mid-cycle review with multiple OKRs teams.
- Integrate OKRs into existing team meetings and reports.

With OKRs published in your client's OKRs tracker, you are ready to coach your client through Step 2, check in and monitor progress. Without a coach, teams often do not integrate OKRs into their daily work.

CONTRIBUTION: **CREATE AN OKRs WORKING AGREEMENT CANVAS**

Madlyn Del Monte, OKRs coach and founder of Agile Gangster LLC

As an OKRs coach, I've observed that some teams that express interest in OKRs do not know what they're signing up for. Many teams define their OKRs but do not integrate OKRs into their daily work. In the OKRs community, we call this "set-it-and-forget-it." One of my clients asked me to develop a working agreement canvas. Teams fill out their canvas and sign it at the bottom. While the canvas can be customized, all include team name, mission, OKRs review cadence, who will attend reviews, and how we celebrate OKRs.

When each team creates their own working agreement and commits to a cadence for reviewing OKRs throughout the cycle, they avoid the set-it-and-forget-it pitfall. I now create a one-page OKRs working agreement canvas for each team member to review and sign at the start of the OKRs cycle. Based on its initial success, I now use this with every team I coach.

While set-it-and-forget-it is the most common pitfall, some teams overcompensate by introducing excessive OKRs-specific check-in meetings for the entire team to attend. In fact, we've seen some organizations introduce two meetings per week just to review OKRs! More meetings can make an OKRs program feel like yet another burden.

The check-in step works best when integrated into existing team meetings. We advise teams to begin their weekly or biweekly team meetings with a quick OKRs review. If you are starting the engagement exclusively with top-level OKRs, you have an advantage. Given that executives often play the role of team lead, your client will be in position to build off their success at the top level when the time comes to explore OKRs at the team level.

If your client wants help with team-level OKRs from the start, we advise narrowing the scope to coaching a small group of three to five pilot teams through a complete OKRs cycle. Remember to leverage the *crawl-walk-run* mantra by emphasizing learning about OKRs during the first cycle and reserving the second cycle to explore how best to scale the program. Regardless of how you start, most organizations will ultimately want your coaching to support team-level OKRs.

There are two types of team-level coaching sessions that you can facilitate to optimize your client's check-in process: (1) single-team sessions with the members of one team deploying OKRs, and (2) multi-team sessions with members of several teams.

Single-Team Check-Ins

Our clients often adopt a standard set of tools for each step of the OKRs cycle. In Step 1, we provide clients with an OKRs drafting template and an OKRs tracker. For Step 2, we help our clients develop a standard check-in tool such as the sample template shown in Figure 5.4.[8]

Nearly all our clients document progress in a standard format in a single location. We recommend that this single location be whatever is most comfortable for your client. For example, this single system might be a dedicated OKRs software solution. However, many of our clients use existing systems such as Google Sheets, Microsoft PowerPoint, or Confluence. Champions provide updates on key results as part of a structured check-in discussion. As a coach, you bring structure to your client's check-in process. You facilitate at least one check-in session with each team deploying OKRs.

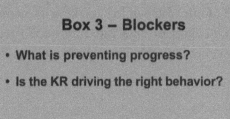

Box 1 – Progress

- How did we do on recent action items to drive the Key Result (KR)?
- Include current value of KR.

Box 2 – Predicted Score

- Enter predicted score/confidence.
- Use selected scoring system.

Box 3 – Blockers

- What is preventing progress?
- Is the KR driving the right behavior?

Box 4 – Action Plan

- List action items to drive the KR.

FIGURE 5.4   Sample 2 × 2 template for OKRs cycle step 2, check in and monitor

CONTRIBUTION: **OPTIMIZE CHECK-INS WITH STRUC-TURED QUESTIONS**

Dikran Yapoujian, first OKRs.com certified coach

When facilitating check-in sessions, it helps to ask structured questions. I begin by asking if we are on track to achieve the key result. *(This is expressed as a probability of achievement by end of period or color-coded with green or red.)*

- **If yes, how do you know?** What gives you confidence we're green or have a probability of x%? (Avoid excessive "progress updates" about recently completed work. Instead, focus on whether we're on track to hit the target.)
- **If not, what's happened to change our confidence?** Where are the blockers? (This might be a conflicting priority, dependency on another team not participating, resources not engaging, or simply a lack of focus on the OKR.)
- **What alternatives have you considered to getting back on track?** (The team should have considered what choices they have – could be redeploy resources, add capacity, clear conflicting priorities, etc.)
- **What is your recommendation?** What decision do you need from this team to proceed? (The team should be prepared to act on the recommendation(s) during the check-in process. That's what allows the OKR framework to add tremendous value, especially for teams not used to acting so nimbly.)

Finally, once we have confidence that key results marked "green" are on track, most clients focus their check-ins on the red items, making check-ins more efficient.

In addition to providing your client with a visual like the one in Figure 5.4 and agreeing on questions to help facilitate single-team check-ins, you must ensure that teams complete the check-in step of the OKRs cycle. As Madlyn Del Monte noted in her working agreement canvas described earlier in this chapter, teams should agree on how often they will review OKRs at the start of the cycle. This cadence can be weekly, biweekly, monthly, or even ad-hoc.

Multi-Team Check-Ins (The Mid-Cycle Review)

If your client has multiple teams setting OKRs, you facilitate a mid-cycle review with multiple teams. Do not allow each team to read through their entire set of OKRs. Apart from top-level OKRs, reading through a complete set of OKRs is a waste of time. Instead, we advise giving each team several minutes to share two key results with the larger group. One key result should be on track—we call this the *big win*. Another key result should not be on track—we call this the *big learn*.

When sharing the big win, key result champions take a couple of minutes to share and celebrate progress, often thanking people outside their team. Some organizations clap after each big-win key result is announced.

When sharing the big learn, key result champions take responsibility, sharing what they are learning about the business and/or the OKRs process itself. This is not a time to point fingers outside the team. We encourage the audience to cheer champions after each big-learn key result is shared. Doing so reinforces that OKRs are about learning in addition to making measurable progress. In addition, clapping can be an effective way to keep the session moving.

Be sure your client has a timekeeper to keep the meeting on track. Mid-cycle reviews with multiple teams are typically planned for an hour. These reviews work best when limited to at most seven teams. If a team needs more than 10 minutes, set up a follow-up discussion with a smaller group. After completing the mid-cycle review, you are ready to move on to the final step of the OKRs cycle, reflect and reset.[9]

 ## STEP 3: REFLECT AND RESET

Pitfalls
■ Skipping this step entirely
■ Conducting a retrospective that only looks back

Solutions

- Schedule reflect and reset sessions with clear agendas.
- Ensure that teams apply learnings to inform next cycle's OKRs.

Reflect and reset is our favorite step in the OKRs cycle. Unlike a retrospective that emphasizes looking back, this step features both a reflection on the past as well as a reset that focuses the team on how best to move forward. Perhaps we like this step so much because we take credit for inventing it! This is where the rubber meets the road. This is your opportunity to help your client build their goal-setting muscle as they apply learnings to inform the next OKRs cycle.

While you do not hold your client accountable for achieving a given key result, you do hold your client accountable for learning. Each team must document learnings from each key result. To optimize learning, consider including two teams in a single reflect and reset session as this allows teams to watch another team complete the process.

Our clients often like to send an email to set expectations about their upcoming reflect and reset coaching sessions. Let's look at an actual email one of our clients sent to each team leader to help prepare for reflect and reset sessions at the end of their first OKRs cycle. Typically, the OKRs project lead sends this email (as shown on following page).

Outcome of the Reflect and Reset Session

Let's analyze the outcome of an actual reflect and reset coaching session for a sample key result. We used our client's OKRs tracker tool to facilitate the session. The tracker included three fields for reflect and reset: (1) Final Score, (2) Learning, and (3) Keep, Modify, or Remove? Figure 5.5 illustrates how we used this tracker for the key result: "Increase partners from 100 to 500."[10]

Sample Email to Announce Step 3 of the OKRs Cycle – Reflect and Reset
When to Send: Two to three weeks prior to the end of an OKRs cycle
Email Subject: Preparing for our upcoming OKRs reflect and reset sessions
From: OKRs Project Lead
To: In this case, it was sent to 12 team leads setting OKRs. However, an email like this may also be sent to an entire group of attendees from the initial OKRs workshop or the entire list of key result champions who will reflect and reset on their key result during the session.
[Email Body:]
All,
As you recall, our OKRs coach helped us get through Step 1: set and align OKRs and Step 2: check in and monitor. As we prepare for the end of our first OKRs cycle, it is time for Step 3: reflect and reset. In this last step of the cycle, we document learnings and draft OKRs for the upcoming quarter.

Timeline for creating OKRs as we enter our next cycle in Q4:
- By Oct 1: Reflect and reset with [COACH NAME]
- By Oct 8: Review draft OKRs with CEO to confirm direction
- By Oct 15: Refine OKRs with [COACH NAME]
- By Oct 22: Publish to the OKRs tracker

Instructions: At the end of each cycle, we take an hour to reflect on the prior period's OKRs and apply what we learned. The outcome of a reflect and reset session is that each key result: (1) gets final scoring, (2) has a documented learning, and (3) is classified into one of three buckets:
1. **Keep:** The key result's final score is not where we want it to be. We need to KEEP focused on moving this metric forward.
2. **Modify:** The key result needs to be adjusted based on learning. For example, we may have set a key result: "$5 million in new customer revenue" and achieved $10 million with a single customer only to learn that we need a more diverse set of customers. In this case, we might MODIFY to "five customers with $1 million+ revenue each."
3. **Remove:** The key result is no longer worth pursuing or is best monitored as a health metric.

All key result champions attend reflect and reset sessions. Other interested team members are encouraged to join as well.
Thanks,
[OKRS PROJECT LEAD NAME]

Key Result	1. Final Score	2. Learning		3. Keep, Modify, or Remove?
Increase partners from 100 to 500 Commit = 200 Target = 300	140; score is **ZERO**	Assumed partners would complete sales themselves given they pay up front. Learned that partners need handholding. Look beyond paid partner sign–ups.		**Modify.** Draft a KR like "Increase 'high quality' partners as measured by 3 certificates sold in first month from X to Y."

FIGURE 5.5 Sample OKRs tracker from step 3, reflect and reset

After reading the key result aloud, the key result champion explained that the key result was scored a zero, shared the learning, and suggested that we apply this learning to draft a modified key result for the next cycle.[11] When the key result was created in Step 1, the team expected to easily double partners from 100 to 200. In fact, 200 partners represented the commit level of progress. We pointed out that this growth rate seemed quite high as a commit, but the team confirmed that they felt anything short of 200 would be considered a failure. They felt 500 would be a stretch and reported a 50% confidence of ending the quarter with 300 partners.

When we started the reflect and reset session, the final score field was already populated with "140 score is ZERO." Midway into the OKRs cycle, they confirmed that it was easy to get more partners, but difficult to get quality partners. The learning field was also populated. The team took a few minutes to apply their learning to draft a key result for the upcoming cycle. Everyone agreed that the focus needed to shift to *quality* rather than *quantity* of partners. As external OKRs coaches, we asked, "What makes a partner 'high quality,' and how can we make this measurable?" In just a few minutes, the team clarified what they meant by a "quality partner" with the magic words "as measured by."

While they did not specify the commit, target, and stretch level of progress during the reflect and reset session, they walked out with a draft key result for the upcoming cycle based on what they had learned in the prior cycle. They learned that new partners who failed to sell certificates right away tended to drop out of the program. They applied this learning to draft a new key result, "Increase high-quality partners as measured by three certificates sold in first month from X to Y."

Ending the cycle with a draft set of OKRs for the next cycle positions your client for success as they begin Step 1 of the next cycle. Here are tips for making the reflect and reset session a success:

- **Purpose.** (1) Agree on final scores for key results, (2) capture learnings from the OKRs cycle, and (3) apply these learnings to the next cycle.
- **Duration.** Depending on the number of key results, 30–60 minutes. Limit the time per key result to 10 minutes. If more time is required, agree who will meet after the group discussion to resolve.
- **Attendees.** Key result champions must attend this session; ideally, the entire team attends. Consider conducting a reflect and reset coaching session with two teams to optimize learning.

OKRs CYCLE COACHING CASE STUDY

Now that we've covered the three steps of the OKRs cycle, let's look at an OKRs coaching case study that follows an OKR through each step. Our client was a high-tech e-commerce company. Let's call this client "Company ABC." Company ABC's leadership was not happy with their existing OKRs program. They felt they had defined too many OKRs and that they were poorly written. Most teams set several objectives and defined well over 10 key results. Many key results looked more like tasks than results.

The leadership team sought to use OKRs to increase focus. The organization was in rapid-growth mode. The CEO felt "everyone worked really hard but had taken on too many projects." They wanted to implement OKRs to get teams to stop chasing the latest shiny object.

Step 1: Set and Align

As with all our clients, we defined deployment parameters prior to getting started with OKRs cycle coaching. Most relevant to this case study, we agreed to limit each team to two objectives and adopted a modified version of the *Radical Focus* approach to scoring. Rather than writing each key result as a target with a 50% confidence level, they opted to define stretch key results with just a 25% confidence level. This case study focuses on the partner success team led by Jimmy. Jimmy quickly developed his team's mission and completed the alignment check step. The final version of the OKR analyzed in this case study is as follows.

Partner Success Team Mission: Make Company ABC a relevant, long-term, value-creating partner for retailers.

Objective: End Q3 on track to retain 90% of last year's total revenue share from existing partners.

Why Now? While it's always important to keep bringing on new partners, retaining existing partners is vital to prove that our business model is viable over the long term. Partners often want to renew at a preferred rate that shifts revenue their way over time. However, if we are creating long-term value, we should be able to preserve our margins on these renewals. Once we have a solid base of partners renewing for multiple years that proves our model is a win-win, we will be in position to easily attract new partners.

Key Results:

1. Retain ALL Top 10 partners up for renewal in Q3 with an overall average of 90% of existing revenue-share agreements.[12]
2. Increase number of Enterprise product approvals or launches from 3 in Q2 to 5 in Q3.
3. Double in-person meetings from 50 in Q2 to 100 in Q3 (each meeting must have next steps that drive KR 1 and/or KR 2 above).

We spent most of our coaching time defining measurable key results. Here is an excerpt of the OKRs coaching dialog between me (external coach) and Jimmy (team lead). This conversation occurred right after drafting the objective and illustrates how we refined three key results at the end of Step 1 of the cycle.

> **OKRs Coach/Ben:** How will we know that we will "end Q3 on track to retain 90% of last year's total revenue share from our existing partners?" How many partners are on board now? Should all be counted the same or are some partners more impactful than others?

> **Partner Success Team Lead/Jimmy:** We have several hundred partners. And yes, some partners are more impactful than others. In fact, for the next few months, we want to focus on the top 10 partners up for renewal. The top 10 make up about 80% of the revenue up for renewal.

> **Ben:** OK, so how can we make this measurable? Is it as simple as either renewing a partner or not renewing a partner?

Jimmy: Kind of, but not quite. We tend to retain nearly every partner. The tricky thing is to renew our partners without giving away too much of the pie. We want to retain partners without losing our revenue share, which is typically set anywhere between 1.5% and 2.5%.

Ben: Are you measuring your ability to renew partners while maintaining revenue share?

Jimmy: Yes, when we figure all our partners into the equation, including the ones we lose for whatever reason, we're coming in at 70% to 90% total partner revenue retention.

Ben: What is the most amazing revenue retention you can imagine in Q3?

Jimmy: 100% is theoretically possible, but nearly impossible since none of the partnerships are set up to increase our revenue share, and some are set to reduce slightly over time. I'd say 90% would be amazing.

Ben: Is that a stretch key result with 25% probability of achievement?

Jimmy: Yes.

→ Leads to key result 1: Retain ALL Top 10 partners up for renewal in Q3 with an overall average of 90% of existing revenue-share agreements.

Jimmy: We need to launch new products based on what our partners want. This shows we're adding more value and being responsive. We need a key result like launch five products in Q3.

Ben: Is that even possible?

Jimmy: Not really. But we could write it as launch – or get approval to launch – five products in Q3.

Ben: Does any product count here?

Jimmy: No. We should count enterprise products only; they are the ones partners are demanding.

Ben: OK, that sounds like a potential key result. Have you measured the number of enterprise products launched in the past, say for last quarter?

Jimmy: Yes. Last quarter we launched two and got approval for one, but our CEO and our partners want more. In our market, launching products creates buzz. In fact, even getting approval to launch means we can make the announcement in a press release. This helps retain as well as attract new partners.

Ben: I hesitate to recommend a key result based simply on the number of launches. A key result should measure the impact of a launch.

Jimmy: I get that, but we will not see the real impact of these launches for quite some time. In fact, we may see some near-term business impact as new products allow us to show partners that we're making progress. This gives us something positive to share when we meet up. By the way, that's really the most important indicator for how partnerships are going. We need to be more proactive with our partners rather than waiting to reach out the month or two before they are up for renewal.

→ Leads to key result 2: Increase the number of enterprise product approvals or launches from 3 in Q2 to 5 in Q3.

Ben: I get that you want to be more proactive. How can we measure your level of proactivity?

Jimmy: It's all about face-to-face partner meetings. We had 50 in Q2. If we could double that, it would be great. One hundred in Q3 would be about 10 per week, assuming 10 full weeks in Q3, which is basically two per week for each of our five key players. It's a stretch, but it's possible.

Ben: We typically do not want key results like "have lots of meetings," as that sounds more like a task. What is the intended outcome of these meetings? Are all meetings equally impactful?

Jimmy: Good question. Some meetings are better than others. The intended outcome is to get to know what's working and what we need to be doing better for our partners.

Ben: OK, can you think of a specific meeting that was highly impactful?

Jimmy: The best meetings have a documented outcome that informs the team.

Ben: And how will this documented outcome inform the team?

Jimmy: When the meeting clearly leads to an action item. It's a good outcome if we get a suggestion from our partner that drives retention or helps shape how we create an enterprise product.

Ben: What about "double in-person meetings from 50 in Q2 to 100 in Q3 that include documented ideas for improving retention or a new product"?

Jimmy: I really like that one! How about we specify that each meeting must have next steps that drive key result 1 and/or key result 2? This will force us to be 100% clear about the goal of our partner meetings before the meeting. And it keeps us focused on our first two key results, which I expect will be our focus for the next OKRs cycle as well. It should really drive accountability.

→ Leads to key result 3: Double in-person meetings from 50 in Q2 to 100 in Q3 (each meeting must have next steps that drive KR 1 and/or KR 2).

Jimmy: Our team drafted a fourth key result, as well: "Create a tangible partner feedback loop that drives enterprise roadmap."

Ben: OK. How will we know that the partner feedback loop drives the roadmap, and how do we know that this is a good thing?

Jimmy: I see your point, let me think about that one a bit more and get back to you for a follow-up session.

Here is the email I sent as follow-up:

Subject: OKRs coaching notes for Jimmy/Partner Success
[Body:]
Hi Jimmy,
Great session just now! Good job thinking about the intended outcome of in-person meetings. Going into these meetings knowing the goal will help ensure they are impactful.

Summary
- Reviewed your OKR
- Modified the objective to reflect the Q3 time frame

Key Takeaways
- Jimmy: For key result 3, rather than simply tracking in-person partner meetings, we count a meeting only when it results in a clear next step that drives key result 1 or 2.
- Ben: Getting approval to launch is just about as valuable as the actual launch itself, so we refined key result 2 to capture this.

Next Steps
- Your fourth key result to create the tangible feedback loop seems like a task. What is the intended outcome of the feedback loop? How will we know this loop is making a positive impact? Feel free to send your refined key result regarding the feedback loop to me for comments.
- Review proposed OKRs with CEO to finalize.
- Publish in OKRs tracker. Stay tuned for details on this!
  —Ben

Step 2: Check In and Monitor

Jimmy met with the CEO to finalize his team's OKRs, and we published these into their OKRs tracker. Just a few weeks later, it was time for a mid-cycle check-in. Jimmy and his team completed the mid-cycle check-in columns from the OKRs tracker, as shown in Figure 5.6.

Jimmy summarized his experience with Step 2, check in and monitor process near the end of the cycle:

Key Result	Key Result Champion	Mid-Period "Actual Score"	Mid-Period "Predicted Score"
1. Retain ALL top 10 partners up for renewal in Q3 with an overall average of 90% of existing revenue-share agreements.	Jimmy	4 of 10 (40%)	80%
2. Increase the number of enterprise product approvals or launches from 3 in Q2 to 5 in Q3.	Miles	1 of 5 (20%)	40%
3. Double in-person meetings from 50 in Q2 to 100 in Q3 (each meeting must have next steps that drive KR 1 and/or KR 2).	Tina	50 of 100 (50%)	80%

FIGURE 5.6 Check-in columns from an OKRs tracker

As point person, we had a tracking sheet just with our three key results. This sheet lived in real time and led to a wild success for our team. We started each team meeting with a quick review of where we were on each key result. So, every team member was aware of these key results and how we were tracking. We challenged each other about the number of meetings completed each week. But it was all done in a productive way that focused and aligned our team.

As the external coach, I joined Jimmy and his team for just one, single-team check-in session. The coaching for this cycle concluded with reflect and reset.

Step 3: Reflect and Reset

Near the end of Q3, I facilitated a reflect and reset coaching session with Jimmy and his fellow key result champions. We started by confirming the final score for each key result. The numerical scores felt somewhat arbitrary, as they did not adopt a prescoring system to specify a 0.3/commit or 0.7/target. Instead, they assigned a number between 0 and 1 based on their understanding of Google's key result grading system. Figure 5.7 summarizes final scores and decisions to keep, modify, or remove. As the text did not fit nicely into the tracker, we inserted comments into each cell. These comments are summarized below the figure.

Key Result	Final Score	Learning	Keep, Modify, or Remove
1. Retain ALL top 10 partners up for renewal in Q3 with an overall average of 90% of existing revenue-share agreements.	1.0	See below	Keep
2. Increase the number of enterprise product approvals or launches from 3 in Q2 to 5 in Q3.	0.3	See below	Modify
3. Double in-person meetings from 50 in Q2 to 100 in Q3 (each meeting must have next steps that drive KR 1 and/or KR 2).	1.0	See below	Remove

FIGURE 5.7   Reflect and reset columns from an OKRs tracker

Key Result 1

- **Score 1.0!** We hit 89.6%, which we're rounding up to 90%.
- **Learning:** This felt almost like a miracle, looking back at it. We do not feel we gamed the system even though I know you are not supposed to achieve the 1.0 level often.
- **Keep.** This is really a big win for us, but I'm afraid if we make this a health metric, we could lose focus. If we maintain 90% next quarter, we might move it out of our OKRs and make it a health metric.

Key Result 2

- **Score 0.3.** We made progress, but we only got halfway there. Even though we launched just one product and got approval for one other, we agreed to score this 0.3 as it does reflect some progress.
- **Learning:** It's much harder than expected to launch enterprise products – or even get approval to do so – in just three months. We did add some major features that delighted our partners on existing products, so we feel like we made some progress. Our other lesson is that we need to make this a dependent key result or even create a shared OKR with the product team. We do not actually launch products within our team. We mostly collect product requests from partners and share those internally and sometimes give feedback on prioritization. Going forward, we need more conversations outside our team. We will review our partner success OKR with dependent teams before finalizing. In general, we should align up front with OKRs that cross teams.
- **Modify.** We will synch up with product team to align on this key result.

Key Result 3

- **Score 1.0!** We somehow ended up with just over a hundred meetings with documented outcomes that drive our first two key results.
- **Learning:** Writing key results in a very tangible and specific way worked well. For example, if we wrote, "100 meetings with our partners," we would not have gotten this much value from the meetings.
- **Remove.** We can monitor this as a health metric next quarter.

Coaching Takeaways

✔ Get a commitment to complete all three steps of the OKRs cycle from every team you coach.

✔ Ensure your client's OKRs tracker enables them to monitor OKRs at each step of the cycle.

✔ Step 1: Set and Align OKRs

  ✔ Apply the seven steps for creating team-level OKRs.

  ✔ Help teams define long-term missions as context for drafting their OKRs.

  ✔ Ensure key results meet each of the eight characteristics of effective key results.

✔ Step 2: Check In and Monitor

  ✔ Populate your client's OKRs tracker with their OKRs for the first cycle.

  ✔ Integrate OKRs into existing team meetings/reports.

  ✔ Conduct a mid-cycle review with an expanded group; keep it short.

✔ Step 3: Reflect and Reset

  ✔ Help clients create an email to announce their first reflect and reset session.

  ✔ Take at most 10 minutes to reflect and reset on each key result.

  ✔ Emphasize learning and drafting OKRs for the next cycle.

NOTES

1. For more on M + OKRs = MOKRs equation, refer to the OKRs.com blog post: MOKRs: OKRs with a Mission https://okrs.com/2015/07/mokrs-okrs-with-a-mission.

2. Frameworks for developing strategy are beyond the scope of this book. For a summary of how missions create context for OKRs, refer to Paul Niven and Ben Lamorte, *Objectives and Key Results: Driving Focus Alignment, and Engagement with OKRs* (Hoboken, NJ: John Wiley and Sons, 2016), pp 42–54.

3. For more on cross-functional squads and functional teams, refer to the first deployment parameter detailed in Chapter 3.

4. For a definition and examples of dependent key results and shared OKRs, refer to Niven and Lamorte, *Objectives and Key Results*, p. 111.

5. We allocated 10 minutes to the alignment check exercise as part of a simulated OKRs coaching session with one team at a recent workshop. However, we ended up dedicating two hours to complete the alignment check exercise. This client created a "dependency matrix" summarizing how various teams depended on one another for the upcoming OKRs cycle. This client reported that the alignment exercise was the most valuable outcome of the workshop.

6. For more sample objectives, refer to the Sample Email with Prework for a Top-Level Workshop section in Chapter 4.

7. The distinction of leading and lagging indicators is nothing new. For more, we recommend the following KPI Library article: https://kpilibrary.com/topics/lagging-and-leading-indicators.

8. This sample template is loosely based on the four-quadrant check-in system described in Christina Wodtke, *Radical Focus: Achieving Your Most Important Goals with Objectives and Key Results* (Boxes and Arrows, 2017), pp. 62–71. Some of our clients create a template like this for each key result; others use a template that captures all key results for a given objective.

9. Additional content from actual mid-cycle OKRs reviews is available to members of the OKRs Coaching Network. For example, we explore how and when to modify or remove key results in the middle of a cycle.

10. Increasing partners was just one of the three key results for our client's objective: "Prove our online partner model is scalable." We advise revisiting objectives after completing Step 3, reflect and reset, for each key result.

11. Recall the three main learning areas from reflect and reset as mentioned in Chapter 2: (1) how to optimize the OKRs program, (2) how to better get stuff done at work, and (3) how best to make a business impact. This key result falls into the third category, how best to make a business impact.

12. Jimmy's first key result did not include a baseline. In this case, we did not write the key result using the "X to Y" format. Questions we might discuss in the OKRs Coach Network about this first key result include: What questions could a coach ask to specify the baseline? Is it critical to define a baseline in this case or is this key result fine without one?

CHAPTER 5 **EXERCISES**

Exercise 5.1: Create and send OKRs coaching emails.
Complete this exercise for each of the three steps in the cycle.
Each email should include: (1) summary, (2) key takeaways, and (3) next steps.

Exercise 5.2: Design an OKRs tracker that captures all three steps of the OKRs cycle.
Load your client's actual OKRs into the tracker and review with your project lead.
Use Figures 5.6 and 5.7 as inspiration.

Epilogue

Your Journey as an OKRs Coach

YOU'VE COMPLETED THE FIRST book to define OKRs coaching. You have the playbook for coaching an organization through the three phases of a structured OKRs engagement. You have the foundation for your journey as an OKRs coach.

We hope the next part of your OKRs journey is application. And this next part of this journey is best done with others. Together, we can take the field of OKRs coaching to the next level through the OKRs Coach Network (www.OKRsCoach.Network). We created this network to bring this book to life and connect with coaches around the world. The network's mission is to enable coaches to connect and exchange best practices to develop OKRs coaching skills that improve alignment, focus, engagement, communication, and learning.

Network members connect with OKRs coaches on our discussion board and participate in Q&A sessions with leading OKRs experts. Members have access to materials such as:

- Sample slides and handouts for OKRs training workshops
- Sample OKRs coaching proposals and work plans
- Coaching email templates to use at each step of the OKRs cycle
- Sample OKRs tracker worksheets

This epilogue previews content from the OKRs Coach Network, including (1) questions OKRs coaches ask, (2) a sample OKRs drafting template, (3) ineffective and effective key results, and (4) two real-world stories that we believe will help you become a better OKRs coach.

QUESTIONS OKRs COACHES ASK

Recall the definition of OKRs – "a critical thinking framework and ongoing discipline that seeks to ensure employees work together, focusing efforts to make measurable contributions." This ongoing critical thinking is about reflection and asking questions. Regardless of your role in an OKRs program, everyone involved should be familiar with the most common questions that comprise this critical thinking framework. The following questions focus on each of the three steps of phase 3, OKRs cycle coaching.

OKRs Cycle Step 1: Set and Align OKRs

Questions about mission
- Whom do we serve? Who is our customer?
- Why do we exist? What is our purpose?
- What do we offer? What is our core offering?
- What is the long-term impact we make?

Questions about alignment
- What teams do we depend on?
- Which teams do we collaborate with most often?
- Which teams depend on us? How?

Questions about objectives
- **Fundamental objective question:** What is the most important area to focus on to make measurable progress in the near term?
- Why is this objective so important? Why now?
- If we could only focus on one objective, what would it be?

Questions about key results (when drafting)
- **Fundamental key result question:** At the end of the period, how will we know "the objective" will be achieved?
- What metric needs to move to make progress on the objective?

Questions to convert tasks into key results (when drafting)

- **Fundamental task-to-key result question:** What is the intended outcome of the task?
- If we complete the task, does that mean we've achieved the objective?
- What is the most amazing outcome you can imagine that could result from completing the task?

Questions about key results (when refining)

- Measurable: Rather than "increase the metric to Y," can we specify where we are now? Can we write in the form "increase the metric from X to Y"?
- Clear: Can any jargon or acronyms be removed or clarified? Would a high school graduate understand the key result?
- Scoring
  - *Stretch:* What is the most amazing outcome you can imagine that is still possible? What level of progress do we feel we have a 10% probability of achieving this period?
  - *Target:* What level of progress do you feel we have a 50% probability of achieving this period?
  - *Commit:* What level of progress can we commit to as a team that we are 90% likely to achieve?
- Key, not all: Is the proposed key result really a focus for improvement or simply business as usual?
- Health metric versus key result: Is the drafted key result already at an acceptable level? If so, is it better classified as a health metric?

Questions to ask when challenging a set of key results (when drafting and refining)

- If all key results are achieved, is the objective also achieved?
- Do the key results reflect the objective? If not, consider modifying the objective or moving the key result to a different objective.
- How can the set of key results be reduced?
- Do the key results capture quantity and quality? Leading and lagging?

OKRs Cycle Step 2: Check In and Monitor

- What is the actual progress right now for this key result?
- What have we done to move the key result?
- What do you predict we will achieve by the end of the cycle?

- Why did your confidence for this key result change?
- What is the risk and how can we mitigate it?
- What is the action plan going forward?
- Is this key result driving the right behaviors?

OKRs Cycle Step 3: Reflect and Reset

- What is the final score for this key result?
- What is the business impact of this key result, looking back on it?
- Was the amount of effort put into moving this key result justified?
- As you think about the upcoming period, do you feel like we should keep, modify, or remove this key result? Why?
- What did we learn about how to deal with dependencies or blockers?
- How can we apply what we learned to OKRs for the next cycle?

SAMPLE OKRs WORKSHOP HANDOUT

The questions in this last section are designed for you, the OKRs coach. The sample handout on the opposite page incorporates these questions into a tool you can use with your clients to draft team-level OKRs. It incorporates our recommended Stretch Target Commit model for scoring key results. We've used it successfully with hundreds of teams to get started with Step 1 of the OKRs cycle. We recommend you do the same.

OKRs DRAFTING TEMPLATE FOR TEAMS

STEP 1: MISSION

Why does our team exist? Whom do we serve? What is the long-term impact we make? *(1 sentence)*

STEP 2: ALIGNMENT CHECK

We depend on these people/teams: _____

These people/teams depend on us: _____

STEP 3A: OBJECTIVE

What is our focus for measurable progress on in the near term? *(1 sentence)*

STEP 3B: *WHY NOW?*

Educate and motivate staff. *(3–5 sentences)*

STEP 4: KEY RESULTS

We will have achieved the objective by end of OKRs cycle as measured by...

Key Result 1: _____

Key Result 2: _____

Key Result 3: _____

Scoring Criteria

Stretch – Most amazing outcome that is still possible. 10% likely to be achieved.

Target – Difficult but attainable. 50% likely to be achieved.

Commit – What we expect to achieve. 90% likely to be achieved.

EXAMPLES OF INEFFECTIVE AND EFFECTIVE KEY RESULTS

Our clients often ask us for help improving the quality of their key results. Therefore, we include a slide showing key results before and after coaching in our training slide decks, as shown in Figure E.1. Use a table like this to demonstrate how your coaching can help make key results more effective. We recommend including at least one of each type of key result to help your client distinguish between metrics, milestones, and baselines.

Type	Ineffective	Effective
Metric	NPS 60+ in Q4	Increase Net Promoter Score (NPS) from current level of 54 in Q3 to 60 in Q4 as reported by new customers within first three months of purchase in the United States. **Stretch:** Increase to 65. **Commit:** Maintain at 54.
Milestone	All teams complete customer interviews	All five functions (product, design, engineering, sales, and customer success) have one or more staff documenting a customer pain point based on a customer interview. **Stretch:** Each of the five functions have documented two customer pain points based on customer interviews. **Commit:** One team member from each of product, design, and engineering have had a conversation with a customer that identifies a pain point.
Baseline	Measure and achieve 90% customer satisfaction	First customer satisfaction survey sent to 100 or more stakeholders with initial results reported based on 20 valid responses. **Stretch:** 80% response rate from first customer satisfaction survey with baseline score reported. **Commit:** Criteria for measuring customer satisfaction is established. List of respondents is identified (expect 100–300 respondents).

FIGURE E.1   Examples of ineffective and effective key results

STORIES FROM THE OKRs COACH NETWORK

Story 1: Value-Focused vs. Alternative-Focused OKRs

When to use this story

- Beginning of Step 1 of the OKRs cycle; use when drafting OKRs.
- Use with clients focused on a list of industry standard metrics or who tend to limit their thinking to the set of metrics already being tracked.

When you order salad, do you think about what you really want in a salad dressing, or do you need to know the choices first? If you ask for the choices first, you're taking an alternative-focused approach to decision-making. Here's the sample conversation I use to illustrate an alternative-focused approach. It's about salad dressing, so almost everyone can relate.

Waiter: "What kind of dressing would you like?"

Me: "What are the options?"

Waiter: "Blue Cheese, Thousand Island, Ranch, or Balsamic."

Me: "OK, Balsamic."

While this may not seem like a major life decision, as I gained weight and started realizing how important it was for me to be alive and healthy when my kids got older, I started taking a value-focused approach. I was eating a lot of salad and wanted to control the amount of oil and reduce my intake of sodium. Here's a different approach to this conversation:

Waiter: "What kind of dressing would you like?"

Me: "Actually, rather than a standard dressing, can you please bring some olive oil and balsamic vinegar on the side?"

I came to the table knowing my values. I used them as the basis for my decision-making. One of my advisors at Stanford, Ralph Keeney, the author of *Value-Focused Thinking*, taught me to distinguish between value-focused and alternative-focused thinking as part of my graduate work in decision analysis.[1] I've applied this distinction to many aspects of my professional and personal life. As I look back on my OKRs coaching sessions, I see a pattern. Effective OKRs coaches help their client focus on values, not just the available alternatives. You may want to share the story below with your client when drafting OKRs at the beginning of Step 1 in the OKRs cycle.

Alternative-Focused Approaches to Drafting OKRs

Let's go back to my first role as a paid external OKRs coach with Hobsons, a leading education software company. Sid Ghatak, VP at Hobsons, played the role of OKRs project lead. To ensure success and give credibility to the project, Sid purchased lists of standard KPIs for each functional area. As directed by Sid, I began my OKRs coaching sessions at Hobsons by presenting standard KPIs as inspiration. For example, I showed the head of HR a list of KPIs from the APQC Process Classification Framework such as "time to fill open positions" and "% of executives with a succession plan" before asking the client to draft OKRs.

I was like a waiter providing a menu of options! I inadvertently forced my client into an alternative-focused approach. I limited their creativity. I was acting more like a consultant rather than a coach. I did not begin by asking questions and taking time to reflect on their knowledge of their own business. By presenting them with a menu, I was positioning myself as the expert. I offered advice rather than inquiry. Two signs that your OKRs drafting process is a broken, alternative-focused exercise are:

1. You are searching online for "standard KPIs or OKRs" for a functional area to use as the basis for drafting OKRs.
2. Your boss, in my case Sid, provides a list metrics and asks teams to select key results based on the metrics provided.

Value-Focused Approaches to Drafting OKRs

Sid and I took some time to reflect on those initial OKRs coaching sessions. We quickly decided to move the list of standard metrics into the appendix of our introductory OKRs coaching slide deck. Thus, we could refer to standard metrics, but only upon request. With this small change, every session was a success. Not a single department manager asked for example metrics!

OKRs coaching should begin with open questions that help your client articulate their most important goals. The process of creating OKRs should be creative. It should reflect your client's values. Begin with questions to solicit objectives: What are the objectives you need to focus on to move toward your long-term mission? What is the single most important objective, and why is it so important right now?

When I brought a list of standard metrics into the coaching session, I initiated an alternative-focused approach. This is an easy mistake to avoid; do not bring in a list of OKRs or metrics into your coaching sessions. Start with a blank slate and ask the fundamental OKRs questions.

However, there is a more subtle form of alternative-focused thinking that occurs when your client limits their thinking to their existing list of KPIs. To fully grasp the danger of this limitation, consider the streetlight story:

> A policeman sees a drunk man searching for something under a streetlight and asks what the drunk has lost. He says he lost his keys, and they both look under the streetlight together. After a few minutes the policeman asks if he is sure he lost them here, and the drunk replies, no, and that he lost them in the park. The policeman asks why he is searching here, and the drunk replies, "this is where the light is."[2]

In the streetlight story, it's as if the metrics you are already tracking are made visible by the light. However, the key results that reflect your objective do not always have great lighting. You must get your client to look in the right place regardless of the lighting. Help your client reflect on their values to enable the right key results to emerge rather than encouraging them to only look at the set of metrics that are already being tracked.

Here is a coaching excerpt with Judy, the VP of a marketing team, that illustrates how to get your client to look deeply into their values rather than simply selecting a key result from a list of existing metrics. This excerpt begins with my client focused only on their alternatives and concludes by showing how a value-focused approach reveals the need to develop a baseline key result.

The alternative-focused dialog is:

OKRs Coach/Ben:	What is the most important area to improve next quarter?
Marketing Director/ Judy:	We need to improve the ROI of our marketing events and campaigns.

Ben:	How will we know at the end of the quarter that we've improved the ROI of our events and email campaigns?
Judy:	Oh, we've got a ton of metrics to measure improvement. For example, click-through rate, bounce-back rates, #unsubscribes, email open rate, time on page ...
Ben:	OK, but we don't need a list of all the things we're currently tracking, we just need a few key results that reflect the near-term improvement.
Judy:	We could go with improve email open rate.
Ben:	What's the current open rate?
Judy:	We're at 3.4%.
Ben:	What would that need to be to represent a real improvement?
Judy:	Are you kidding me, 3.4% is amazing. We just need to maintain it above 3%. Even 2% would be well above the industry benchmark, which is closer to 1.5%.
Ben:	OK, then this is a health metric, not a key result, as OKRs are about improvement, not maintenance.

So far, Judy is focused on the metrics she is already tracking. As the conversation continues, notice how we shift to a more value-focused approach:

Judy:	Makes sense. What we really need to improve is the ROI of marketing events, not just the emails we send out.
Ben:	How will we know if we've improved the ROI of these events?
Judy:	We don't really have metrics for that; it's complicated to measure.
Ben:	Can you think of one successful event and measure the ROI just for that one event?
Judy:	Sure, but we'd need to have the ROI for five or ten events to really get value. We don't even have a definition for the ROI of an event.
Ben:	If it's important, shall we establish a baseline to reflect the ROI of marketing events?

Judy: Yes, but I don't want to waste time trying to measure ROI for all events. We should focus this only on major events.

Ben: OK, how do you define a major event?

Judy: I'd say an event that has a total cost of over $25,000.

Ben: Would that include the time your team dedicates to the event?

Judy: Let's call it $50,000 and make it the fully loaded cost, including overhead.

Ben: OK, how many major marketing events do you think you can report the ROI for over the next quarter?

Judy: Three easily. Ten would be amazing.

Ben: Here's how I think we might translate this into a stretch key result: "Establish a baseline of the ROI of marketing events based on ten major marketing events. Major event = $50,000 + fully loaded cost."

Judy: Yes, that's what I'm suggesting; we should have that one.

The alternative-focused approach limited our thinking to the set of metrics Judy already had on her dashboard. When we shifted to a value-based approach, we realized that what really mattered was not captured in the existing metrics. Therefore, based on our values, we set a key result to obtain a baseline to reflect the return on investment of high-priced marketing events.

Coaching Takeaways

✔ An alternative-focused approach may limit clients to the set of metrics that are already being tracked.
✔ A value-focused approach can make Step 1 of the cycle more effective and may help your client develop baseline key results.

Story 2: Using Baseline Key Results: Net Promoter Score Case Study

When to use this story

▪ End of Step 1 of the OKRs cycle
▪ Especially when refining baseline key results

I was coaching a small, established software company that was not yet measuring Net Promoter Score (NPS). NPS was a popular metric to start tracking back in 2014. I attended an executive briefing in which a leading consulting company presented a benchmark analysis ranking the NPS of my client's competitors. After seeing this presentation, the CEO demanded that the customer success team start monitoring and reporting NPS, so we could see where we stack up and make improvements to beat the competition.

In 2014, I had not yet developed the Stretch Target Commit prescoring system. Thus, our key result was simply "Establish a baseline to report Net Promoter Score." The engineering, marketing, and customer success teams worked together to collect the NPS from two hundred of the one thousand total active customers. They put in a lot of work adding the NPS survey into their software tool and asking their customers to complete NPS surveys. The staff that collected NPS from 20% of their install base was shocked and disappointed when the VP of customer success presented their OKRs status at the company all-hands meeting. When the VP got to the NPS key result, he announced:

> **VP:**   *Well, we didn't get the baseline for NPS. We only had two hundred valid responses, so we'll just collect more data on that one next quarter.*

I could tell the staff that put in the work to collect the data for NPS was dejected. I approached the VP after the meeting:

> **Ben:**   *How many data points do you feel are required to establish a baseline?*
>
> **VP:**   *I don't know, but a lot more than two hundred!*

The next week we drafted OKRs for the next cycle. At this session, we agreed to modify this baseline key result to be more specific and measurable as follows:

Key result: Increase sample size of Net Promoter Score (NPS) metric from 200 to 400 customers and report baseline to benchmark us against the competition. (At start of Q2, we have ~1000 customers. 400 translates to ~40% of our install base.)
  Stretch: Report a solid baseline NPS with 500 customer responses.
  Commit: Report preliminary baseline NPS with 250 customer responses.

I share this story to illustrate the importance of writing key results that are specific and measurable. Even though it is technically a baseline key result, as we don't yet have the metric in place, the baseline can be made measurable simply by specifying the number of data points required to "establish a baseline." Going into the next quarter, the entire team was clear about the criteria for reporting a baseline NPS. We would call it a *preliminary baseline* if we ended the quarter with 250 total customers, a "baseline" if we reached 400 total customers, and a "solid baseline" once we hit 500.

Coaching Takeaways

✔ A draft key result like "Establish a baseline for NPS" needs to be refined; it is not measurable, therefore its achievement is subject to opinion.

✔ When refining baseline key results, specify the number of data points or the measurement period required to "establish a baseline."

 NOTES

1. For more, see Ralph L. Keeney, *Value-Focused Thinking: A Path to Creative Decisionmaking* (Cambridge, MA: Harvard University Press, 1996).
2. Streetlight effect, Wikipedia, https://en.wikipedia.org/wiki/Streetlight_effect.

EPILOGUE EXERCISE **WRITE AN OKRS COACHING STORY FOR OTHER COACHES**

Include three sections:

1. ***When to use the story.*** As I did with the stories above, provide a couple sentences to describe when a coach should consider using your story. If your story relates to Phase 1, specify the relevant deployment parameter(s). If it relates to Phase 2, specify the type of training workshop. If your story relates to Phase 3, specify the step of the OKRs cycle.
2. ***The story itself.*** Use an informal tone, as if you were writing in a personal diary. Reflect on a mistake you made as an OKRs coach. Explain what you learned from the mistake. Limit your story to two thousand words.
3. ***Coaching takeaway.*** Summarize your recommendation for OKRs coaches in a few sentences. Explain how you suggest OKRs coaches incorporate your learning into their practice.

Bonus: Submit your story to Ben@OKRs.com for feedback and possible inclusion in the next edition of this book!

Appendix

 ANSWERS TO QUESTIONS FROM THE INTRODUCTION

Think of the brief answers to the questions from the introduction as a preview of the ongoing discussions we hope to have with you on the OKRs Coach Network discussion board.

1. How can we scale OKRs across a large organization with hundreds of departments? Google is a massive organization and is the most well-known company that uses OKRs today. However, the success at Google does not help answer this question. Google started using OKRs back when they had just under 40 employees on staff. The real question we want to address is, "Can a large company introduce OKRs, and how best can they deploy the system?" Zalando, FlipKart, and Sears Holding Company are three well-documented case studies that prove it's possible to deploy OKRs on a massive scale.[1]

Mantra: The *crawl-walk-run* mantra is critical when scaling OKRs at large organizations. Take a phased approach by deploying OKRs within a specific area before attempting to scale OKRs. In this way, you apply learnings along the way. You nail it before you scale it.

Analysis: Zalando's phased approach worked well. Zalando, a company of about 7,000 employees at the time, dedicated a full year to get OKRs working within their Brand Solutions group. After completing a successful OKRs program within this one group, Zalando introduced OKRs at the company and business unit levels. Finally, Zalando rolled out OKRs at the team level. My experience with Zalando as their external OKRs coach suggests that their systematic rollout was one of the keys to their success with OKRs.

Sears and FlipKart have well over 25,000 employees. Both deployed OKRs at the team level much more quickly than Zalando. Rapid deployments in massive organizations are challenging. However, both Sears and Flipkart had mandates from leadership to deploy OKRs across the entire company on a fast track. Niket Desai, the OKRs project lead at FlipKart, offers the following tip for OKRs coaches based on his experience: "Start at the highest level and slowly go down levels for OKRs instead of all at once."

Often, a large company will only deploy OKRs within certain areas of their business. Several of our larger clients such as Capital One, Nike, and Walmart, leverage OKRs within certain divisions and teams, but do not define OKRs across their entire organization.

2. How can we set team-level OKRs to ensure cross-functional alignment rather than simply using the org chart to define the teams that will set OKRs? Unfortunately, there is no succinct and definitive answer to this question. We recommend reading and rereading Chapter 3 and focusing on the first deployment parameter.

Mantras: The *crawl-walk-run* and *less is more* mantras are critical here. Begin with a small set of teams and define a small number of OKRs to explore what works best for your client. Provide your client with options and consider piloting cross-functional teams after completing your first cycle.

3. How can infrastructure teams such as legal, human resources, and finance benefit from OKRs? Infrastructure teams often benefit by defining OKRs for their team when they are focused on internal improvement. For example, we've seen finance teams benefit from OKRs by defining their team's objective as "streamline repetitive processes to free up more time for analysis" with key results like "reduce average time to close the books each month from two weeks to one."

Many infrastructure teams do not find it valuable to develop OKRs for their own team. However, these same teams often benefit from OKRs by participating in OKRs drafting sessions with their key stakeholders. For example, a legal team may identify the sales team as a key stakeholder for the upcoming OKRs cycle. The legal team may provide input that informs the sales team's OKRs. In doing so, the legal team might even add a name from legal to co-champion a sales team's key result to address a critical dependency.

4. How do we integrate OKRs into our performance management system? As an OKRs coach, you help your client discover their answer. If your client has a performance management system, review the content from the seventh deployment parameter in Chapter 3 with your OKRs project and HR leads. Here are two principles:

- *Do* include OKRs in performance review discussions via structured questions to position managers as coaches.
- *Do not* use scores on key results as the basis for calculating incentive compensation.

5. How do OKRs compare with KPIs? Each organization must find their own answer to this question. We often allocate an entire deployment coaching session to address this topic with our clients in Phase 1. An analysis detailing how OKRs compare with KPIs is covered in the eighth deployment parameter in Chapter 3. We recommend working with each client to design a table based on the comparison of key results and KPIs as shown in Figure 3.5.

6. When do OKRs *not* add value? In our experience, OKRs do not always add value. Let's explore this question from both the company and team level.

Analysis for company level: OKRs do not add value at the company level when the organization is in maintenance mode. Here is a personal story to make this concrete. I live just an hour away from Napa Valley in California. So, it should come as no surprise that I've been asked to present OKRs to a family-run winery. The winery was hitting about $10 million in annual sales and making a small profit each year. Over a glass of wine, the executive team and I reviewed the mission and set some objectives. However, the OKRs we drafted all looked like "health metrics." That is, we did not want to grow the business. We simply wanted to keep things the way they were.

As OKRs are about focusing on areas to make measurable improvement, we concluded that an OKRs deployment would not be a good fit for the winery. Then, we uncorked a couple bottles and celebrated. After all, we were quickly able to make the decision not to do OKRs, so why not celebrate that success? This was one of my most successful "nonclient" case studies, as we avoided wasting time setting OKRs and the wine was excellent.

Analysis for team level: It is often challenging to know whether OKRs will be effective for a given team. In fact, one of my larger tech clients based in the Silicon Valley asked us to conduct a one-year pilot program with five newly formed teams that were in discovery mode. Midway through the pilot, our client decided that only one of the five teams would continue with OKRs. Their key results looked like "hire staff" and "run experiments." This pilot program led to the following two insights about when teams should avoid OKRs:

1. ***Team is not yet formed.*** You know this is a problem when all key results look like "Hire the team as measured by filling X positions by end of period." This is more of a task than a key result.
2. ***Team is purely in discovery mode.*** You know this is a problem when all OKRs look like "run experiments" or "test the market." It's difficult to increase metric A from X to Y when we don't know what metric A should be in the first place!

We find these two insights apply to other organizations as well. Thus, we advise you to be wary of defining team-level OKRs if a team is not yet formed or is purely in discovery mode.

7. How do we ensure that OKRs reflect team thinking rather than orders from the boss? Most objectives are set by leadership. Most key results are defined by team members. We recommend that teams avoid the temptation to define team-level OKRs by simply copying and pasting from higher-level OKRs. Refer to the ninth and tenth deployment parameters from Chapter 3 for more.

8. How do we avoid OKRs that look like a "to-do list"? Writing OKRs as a to-do list is a common pitfall that teams encounter when defining OKRs. Drafting OKRs that look like a to-do list is not necessarily a bad thing. However, publishing OKRs that look like a to-do list misses the point. While some coaches solve this problem by requiring every key result be defined as a metric, we do not advise you to completely abandon milestone key results. Milestones can be effective in some cases as detailed in the fifth deployment parameter of Chapter 3.

As an OKRs coach, you ask questions to help your client translate draft key results that often look a list of tasks into effective key results. You guide your client through a series of questions to design effective key results that reflect measurable outcomes. You ask the fundamental task-to-key-result question: "What is the intended outcome of the task?" To help your client avoid key results that look like a to-do list, review the seven steps for creating team-level OKRs in Chapter 5 and the examples of ineffective and effective key results described in Figure E.1 of the Epilogue.

9. What if some employees do not see how they contribute to company-level OKRs?
If your client asks you this question, get to the underlying concern. Is the concern that leadership wants everyone to feel their work is valued? If so, remind your client that OKRs are not meant to capture all important work across the organization.

Leadership teams that want to capture all important work often present a broader framework as context for OKRs. For example, they may present collectively exhausted categories such as the four perspectives of a balanced scorecard.

We've also seen organizations communicate OKRs in conjunction with health metrics. By reviewing health metrics and OKRs, employees should be able to connect their work to the bigger picture. They should be able to see how their efforts maintain a health metric or move a key result forward. Kuang Yang's contribution at the end of Chapter 3 illustrates how Huawei allows employees to connect their work to both health metrics and OKRs.

To monitor how they connect their work to top-level OKRs, employees often incorporate OKRs into 1:1s with their managers. Some employees may be perfectly fine working on projects that do not connect to company-level OKRs. Perhaps they are focused on maintaining health metrics or completing compliance activities. Other employees may feel a need to contribute to company-level OKRs and therefore may need to adjust their priorities or even their role within the organization to be engaged at work.

10. How do I facilitate an executive workshop to draft top-level OKRs? As with all workshops, be sure to design a structured agenda and run it by the OKRs project lead and executive sponsor. Be ready to depart from the planned agenda as illustrated by the ACME Homes case study. For this case study along with a playbook to help you design, prepare, and facilitate an executive workshop to draft top-level OKRs, refer to the first application section of Chapter 4.

 ## THE FIVE OKRs COACHING MANTRAS

We've embedded five mantras into this book. They are based on our collective coaching experience with hundreds of organizations. Organizations that follow these mantras consistently experience more success with OKRs than those that do not. Here is each mantra with a brief description:

1. *Less is more.* Define a small set of OKRs.
2. *Crawl-walk-run.* Deploy OKRs piecemeal. Begin with pilot teams rather than a full-scale deployment across an entire organization.
3. *Outcomes, not output.* Write key results that mostly reflect outcomes (results) rather than output (amount of work delivered).
4. *OKRs are not everything.* Write OKRs that reflect the most important areas to make measurable progress rather than attempting to reflect everything you do. Distinguish OKRs from tasks and health metrics.
5. *The only way to learn OKRs is to do OKRs.* Allocate most of an OKRs training workshop to drafting your client's real OKRs rather than discussing theory and presenting OKRs from other organizations.

We hope that you live by these mantras. Incorporate them into every OKRs coaching engagement and you are on the path to success!

 NOTE

1. These three case studies are detailed in Paul Niven and Ben Lamorte, *Objectives and Key Results: Driving Focus Alignment, and Engagement with OKRs* (Hoboken, NJ: John Wiley and Sons, 2016), Chapter 7.

Glossary

Advocacy Stating one's views. Describing what I think, disclosing how I feel, expressing a judgment, urging a course of action, and giving an order are all forms of advocacy. *See also*, the analysis of the definition of OKRs coaching at the beginning of Chapter 1.

Alignment Check One of the seven recommended steps for creating team-level OKRs in which a team identifies external dependencies prior to drafting objectives. *See also*, the analysis of "Check Alignment" from the seven steps for creating team-level OKRs in Chapter 5.

Baseline Key Result A type of key result that is used when the current value of a metric that reflects progress of an objective is unknown. The baseline key result establishes X, so that a metric key result to move from "X to Y" can be used in a future OKRs cycle. *See also*, the second story in the Epilogue.

Bottom-Up Originating with input from team members, not by leadership mandate. As a rule of thumb, most key results should be bottom-up. *See also*, the tenth universal deployment parameter in Chapter 3.

Certified OKRs.com Coach While there are many certification programs available to OKRs coaches, certified OKRs.com coaches complete a rigorous program under the supervision of Ben Lamorte and the OKRs.com team. *See also*, the OKRs Coach Network for the latest developments on OKRs.com certification opportunities at: www.OKRsCoach.Network.

Check In and Monitor Step 2 of the OKRs cycle in which a structured conversation occurs within a single OKRs team or multiple teams. These structured conversations are designed to ensure teams focus on OKRs throughout the cycle and avoid the set-it-and-forget-it pitfall. *See also*, the analysis of Step 2 of the OKRs cycle in Chapter 5.

Coachee A person being coached in a coaching session.

Crawl-Walk-Run One of the five OKRs coaching mantras that emphasizes the importance of taking a piecemeal approach when deploying OKRs. Specifically, we advise beginning with pilot teams rather than a full-scale deployment across an entire organization and delaying the purchase of dedicated

OKRs software until completing at least two OKRs cycles. *See also*, the summary of the five coaching mantras in the Appendix.

Critical Thinking In the first part of the definition of OKRs, we use "critical thinking" to reflect the deep listening and set of questions an OKRs coach asks as they guide their client through an OKRs cycle. Here is a more formal definition: "The intellectually disciplined process of actively and skillfully conceptualizing, applying, analyzing, synthesizing, and/or evaluating information gathered from, or generated by, observation, experience, reflection, reasoning, or communication, as a guide to belief and action." *Source:* Scriven & Paul, as presented at the 8th Annual International Conference on Critical Thinking and Education Reform. *See also*, Chapter 1, "What Is OKRs Coaching?"

Cycle Time A quarter by default, "cycle time" refers to the amount of time between the start and end of an OKRs cycle. As noted in the Introduction, many organizations are shifting to a four-month cycle time. *See also*, the fourth deployment parameter in Chapter 3.

Deployment Parameters A given organization's answers to the questions that must be answered before deploying OKRs. *See also*, Chapter 3.

Executive Sponsor The most senior person involved in an OKRs program. *See also*, the executive sponsor role in Chapter 2.

External OKRs Coach A person who provides OKRs coaching to support their client through the three phases of an OKRs coaching engagement. *See also*, the external OKRs coach role in Chapter 2.

Health Metric A metric that is actively tracked and monitored but is not the focus for near-term improvement. Any KPI that is not classified as a key result is often classified as a health metric. *See also*, the eighth deployment parameter in Chapter 3.

Human Resources Lead (HR Lead) A member of your client's HR team who agrees to play a role in an OKRs coaching engagement primarily to ensure that there is no conflict between OKRs and performance management and evaluation. *See also*, the HR lead role in Chapter 2.

Inquiry Asking a question. With genuine questions, the speaker seeks information. Rhetorical or leading questions are a kind of advocacy in disguise. We advise balancing advocacy with inquiry. Unlike consultants who tend to advise their clients, coaches emphasize inquiry, especially during Phase 3, OKRs cycle coaching. *See also*, Chapter 1, "What Is OKRs Coaching?"

Internal OKRs Coach An employee of an organization who provides coaching to help their organization sustain an OKRs program. While internal OKRs coaches may contribute during the first two phases, they focus on the third phase, OKRs cycle coaching. *See also*, the internal OKRs coach role in Chapter 2.

Key Performance Indicator (KPI) A metric that someone, often in a leadership role, feels is important to monitor. A KPI is often used to evaluate the value delivered by the company, a team, and/or a given employee. *See also*, the eighth deployment parameter in Chapter 3.

Key Result One of the measurable statements that defines the achievement of a given objective. Key results answer the question, "How will we know we've made measurable progress on a specific objective by a certain date?" *See also*, Figure E.1 in the Epilogue for examples of ineffective and effective key results.

Key Result Champion A critical role in any OKRs program, key result champions manage the progress of a given key result throughout the OKRs cycle. Some organizations prefer *key result manager* or *key result lead*. *See also*, the key result champion role in Chapter 2.

Key Result Scoring A system for managing expectations and communicating progress (actual and/or predicted) of a key result. Scoring may occur at any of the three steps in the OKRs cycle. Scoring methods include: (1) Radical Focus: key results begin with a 5/10 confidence score, (2) Measure What Matters: key results are classified as either commit or aspirational, and (3) Stretch Target Commit: key results include stretch and commit levels in addition to a target. *See also*, the third deployment parameter in Chapter 3.

Lagging Indicator A type of metric that is difficult to impact in the near term. Also known as *outputs*, leading indicators often reflect financials such as revenue and profit. A set of key results often includes a mix of leading and lagging indicators. *See also*, Step 6 of the seven steps for creating team-level OKRs in Chapter 5.

Leading Indicator A type of metric that is relatively easy to impact in the near term. Leading indicators are often referred to as *inputs* because they are expected to impact a lagging indicator (output) and ultimately impact bottom-line financials. *See also*, Step 6 of the seven steps for creating team-level OKRs in Chapter 5.

Left-Hand Column (LHC) Exercise A technique developed by Dr Chris Argyris, Professor Emeritus at Harvard Business School, to help people reflect on assumptions during a conversation. This exercise is also featured in *The Fifth Discipline Fieldbook*, by Peter Senge. We advise OKRs coaches to adopt this exercise to reflect on coaching sessions to improve learning. *See also*, the two coaching excerpts in Chapter 1 for examples.

Metric Key Result A type of key result that is written in the form "increase (or decrease) a given metric from X to Y" where X represents the current value of the metric and Y represents a desired value of the metric to be reached by the end of a given OKRs cycle period. *See also*, the fifth deployment parameter in Chapter 3.

Milestone Key Result A type of key result that reflects binary outcomes and does not require numbers. *See also*, the fifth deployment parameter in Chapter 3.

Mission A sentence that answers the following four questions for a company or a given team: (1) Why do we exist? (2) Whom do we serve? (3) What is our core offering? (4) What is the long-term impact we make? *See also*, step one of the seven steps for creating team-level OKRs in Chapter 5.

Objective A statement beginning with a verb that answers the question, "Where shall we focus our efforts to make measurable progress in the near term?" Objectives may be classified as internal or external. *Internal objectives* are about improving within the organization. *External objectives* are aimed at making an impact outside the organization. *See also*, step three of the seven steps for creating team-level OKRs in Chapter 5 and the second deployment parameter in Chapter 3.

OKRs Coaching Partnering with clients in a thought-provoking, creative, and structured process over three phases. **Phase 1: deployment coaching** to align on the answers to the questions that define an OKRs program and define the roles and resources that will support the OKRs program. **Phase 2: training** to ensure a shared understanding of OKRs. **Phase 3: cycle coaching**, inquiry that enables a client to critically reflect throughout the three steps of an OKRs cycle to (1) align on where and why to focus effort to make measurable improvement, (2) communicate and monitor progress, and (3) document and apply learnings to the next OKRs cycle. *See also*, "What Is OKRs Coaching" in Chapter 1.

OKRs Coordinator The "taskmaster" of an OKRs program, the OKRs coordinator helps keep their organization's OKRs program on track. *See also*, the OKRs coordinator role in Chapter 2.

OKRs Cycle A recurring, three-step process that starts with (1) setting OKRs, continues with (2) checking-in and monitoring, and concludes with (3) reflect and reset. *See also*, the playbooks for each step of the OKRs cycle in Chapter 5.

OKRs Cycle Time Your client's answer to, "What amount of time will we use to mark the beginning and end of an OKRs cycle?" While a three-month quarter is the default, some organizations do not adopt a quarterly cycle time. For example, as noted in the trends from the Introduction, some teams are moving to a four-month cycle time. *See also*, the fourth deployment parameter in Chapter 3.

OKRs Drafting Template A set of questions that provide a structured approach for a given organization to develop their OKRs. OKRs drafting templates always include "Objective" and "Key Result," and we recommend including additional context such as "Mission" and "Alignment Check." *See also*, the sample drafting handout in the Epilogue.

OKRs Project Lead One of the critical roles in an OKRs program who serves as the primary client contact point for the OKRs coach. Organizations often have two project leads. *See also*, the OKRs project lead role in Chapter 2.

OKRs Review Cadence The frequency at which a given team agrees to review their OKRs. Often weekly, biweekly, or monthly teams review their OKRs at least once during each OKRs cycle. *See also*, the detailed playbook for OKRs cycle coaching in Chapter 5.

OKRs Team A team that defines a set of OKRs, typically within the context of top-level OKRs and/or their organization's strategy. *See also*, the first deployment parameter in Chapter 3.

OKRs Team Lead The person managing a given OKRs team. *See also*, the OKRs team lead role in Chapter 2.

OKRs Team Member Everyone on an OKRs team except the team lead. *See also*, the OKRs team member role in Chapter 2.

OKRs Tracker A single location in which OKRs are stored throughout the three steps of the OKRs cycle. This tracker ensures that there is one place to: (1) publish OKRs, (2) check in and monitor progress, and (3) document final scores and learnings to reflect and reset at the end of each OKRs cycle. *See also*, the case study at the end of Chapter 5.

OKRs Training Workshop An interactive event that covers (1) basic theory of OKRs, (2) why and how the organization is deploying OKRs, and (3) practice applying concepts to develop OKRs and/or train internal coaches to support their organization's OKRs program. *See also*, the three types of OKRs training workshops detailed in Chapter 4.

Refined OKRs A set of OKRs ready for final review with leadership. A set of refined OKRs must have at least one key result champion associated with each key result. Unlike draft key results that often have placeholder numbers (e.g., increase revenue from X to Y), refined key results include actual numbers (e.g., increase revenue from $3 million to $4 million). *See also*, the last three of the seven steps for creating team-level OKRs in Chapter 5.

Reflect and Reset Step 3 of the OKRs cycle in which key result champions document learnings and apply these learnings to inform future OKRs. *See also*, the last two sections in Chapter 5.

Top-Down Originating with leadership, often with minimal or no input from lower-level team members. Most, if not all, objectives should be top-down. *See also*, the ninth and tenth deployment parameters in Chapter 3.

Why Now? A three- to five-sentence answer to the question, "Why is the given objective so important right now?" The explanation of "Why now?" is intended to educate and motivate the staff. *See also*, the sample objectives in Chapter 5 and the fifth trend in the Introduction.

About the Contributors

Kuang Yang has worked for Huawei, a leading company in China, for more than 13 years. He is credited with introducing Huawei to OKRs. In addition to playing the roles of OKRs project lead and internal coach, he developed the OKRs platform that Huawei uses today. After translating *Objectives and Key Results* into Chinese, Kuang wrote the most popular book in Chinese on OKRs, *Performance Empowerment: Beyond OKRs*. He has introduced OKRs to dozens of other Chinese companies, including Alibaba, Tap4fun, SANY, and BGI. Kuang is the first true OKRs practitioner in China.

Dikran Yapoujian is an award-winning corporate executive and advisor with 25 years of experience helping organizations make the most of their strategic planning investment. His professional career spans financial planning and analysis, business strategy, human resources, and operations. After connecting with Ben Lamorte in 2017, Dikran became the first certified OKRs.com coach, where he has helped dozens of teams deploy OKRs. His OKRs clients range from startups to leading global brands such as Audible and Kohler. He enjoys implementing OKRs with organizations looking for a significant lift in strategic execution as they move to a more nimble and proactive decision-making process.

Madlyn Del Monte has led OKRs transformations at Dun & Bradstreet and CBS. After graduating from Queens College with a degree in art and drama, Madlyn spent eight years at Deloitte. She is now an Agile Gangster and the founder of Agile Gangster, LLC. In addition to Agile tools, Agile Gangsters blend Lean, Project Management, and good old-fashioned street smarts to come up with solutions that meet the needs of business partners, not the needs of a framework. Gangsters drive transformation and have a wide network. "Gangster" stands for: **G**oals & OKRs, **A**gile, **N**ext (fail fast), **G**rateful, **S**trategy, **T**ransition, **E**verybody, and **R**espect.

Index